"Every day I get to wake up to a mira
remarkable woman I've ever met. Th
fall in love with her. They always sa,
beautiful on the inside is she is on the outside.' Not only is she stun-
ningly gorgeous, but she's genuinely godly. When you read her story
you will hardly be able to believe it's true. What she went through
was horrific, and for her to come through it unscarred is a miracle.
My wife is a living, breathing, beautiful miracle. My favorite part of
the journey has been to hear Heather talk about her past as if it never
even happened. All over the nation I have told people, 'You know
God has delivered you when you share your testimony and it feels as
if you're talking about another person.' I got to experience her transformation firsthand. I got to disciple my wife the first two years we
knew each other. The truth is, she has been discipling me ever since.
I didn't save Heather. She saved me. Let her story help save you."

Landon Schott
Husband to Heather Schott
Founder of The Rev Ministries and REVtv
Austin, TX

"The power of the gospel is not only found in a perfect God sending
His perfect Son into a lost world. The power of the gospel — the good
news — is that God allows us to partner in His redemptive work to
be lights to those around us. The best "lights" I've ever known were
people broken by bad choices, disqualified by men, and marginalized
as unfit for the Master's use. But our God specializes in changing the
narrative of broken lives and He restores even the most seemingly
hopeless situations. God looks for scarred people who have been
through trials to prove His Word! What Heather Schott has done in
her powerful new book is share her story in a way that inspires, stirs,
and ultimately transforms the reader. Only God can heal. Only God
can restore. Only God can take the cuts of the past and bring you tri-
umphantly into your destiny — unscarred."

John Gray
Associate Pastor, Lakewood Church
Houston, TX

"Heather Schott takes the reader on a heart-wrenching journey from heartbreak and self-destructive behavior to restoration and renewed hope. Her life is a powerful testimony of the redemptive power of God's grace. This book will make the reader feel her pain, understand her disillusionment, and rejoice in her ultimate breakthrough. To see how she has been saved from a life of pain and suffering, and to think of the amazing woman of God she has come to be, there is no question of the presence of the Lord throughout all her trials. *Unscarred* is a wonderful read, and it proves without a doubt that no life is beyond saving through the grace and mercies of Jesus Christ. I am so proud of Heather and the life she has made for herself. I would recommend this book to those who are feeling lost and hopeless as well as those who have a strong will and self-confidence; it is a testament to the power of our Lord and the amazing miracles He performs every day."

Pastor Matthew Barnett
Cofounder of the Dream Center
Los Angeles, CA

"As I read this powerful book, *Unscarred*, by my friend Heather Schott, I was deeply stirred. I immediately realized that this book is a must-read for this generation. I have personally seen the devastation and despair on this generation due to culture, family, and decisions. This book is transformational from cover to cover. Every page screams 'Hold on! There is a better way!' The enemy's number one goal is to mark this generation with a tombstone of despair, while Jesus came to give us an abundant life of power. Heather takes us on a journey of pain, loss, bitterness, and fear, then right into the arms of a Savior who offers redemption, forgiveness, and grace. You will learn that regardless of where you have come from or what you have been through, you can rise to the top at the feet of a loving Savior! Get this book! Pass it around! In doing so, you will receive the award of watching lives walk in freedom. All I can say is, 'Bravo!'"

Pat Schatzline,
International Evangelist, Remnant Ministries International
Birmingham, AL, and author of *Why Is God So Mad at Me?*, *I Am Remnant!*, and *Unqualified*

"In a time in our nation when young women are bombarded with conflicting messages about what it is to be a woman, God is raising up a powerful and pure voice in the life of Heather Schott. Her life story is one of the most glorious pictures of redemption and restoration I know! *Unscarred* is a clear signpost pointing this generation toward the power of redemption in the cross. Every heart that reads it will find in its pages the courage to lean into the cross, leave his or her past behind and move into his or her destiny!"

Laura Zavala Allred
Founder of Standard Bearers International and
the Back To Life Movement, Dallas, TX

"Loved but left lonely, hope turned to hurt, scathed by society, shattered by struggles, left with the aftereffects of battle. We overlook the possibility of healing for our deep emotional wounds and assign ourselves the penalty of eternal scars. This book is real life, genuine, inspiring, and uplifting. Each and every story will regenerate your spirit, captivate your heart, and reprogram your mind, reminding you there is a curative agent for all human hurt . . . Jesus."

Christy Johnson
Copastor Fearless LA Planet Shakers Church
Los Angeles, CA

"This beautifully written book will cause you to laugh, cry, hope again, and trust again. As you read it your faith will be strengthened. It's a reminder of God's unending love and passionate pursuit of us! This book will be a lifeline for so many. Well done, Heather Schott!"

Rachel Campbell
Copastor, Wave Church LA, Los Angeles, CA

"Heather Schott has a powerful, life-changing testimony that causes faith to leap within everyone who hears it! I believe she has a 'right now' voice for her generation and I am honored to know her."

Chris Gilkey
Lead Pastor, Reach Church, Austin, TX

Unscarred

Heather Schott

Unscarred
Heather Schott

Copyright © 2015 Heather Schott

Famous Publishing
Spokane, Washington

ISBN: 978-1-940243-78-8

Library of Congress Control Number: 2015939283

ACKNOWLEDGMENTS

Thank you to my husband who has always pushed me beyond my comfort zone and listened to the voice of God over my life, even when I did not. You have always believed in me and seen the best in me, even when I was at my worst. I would not be who I am today without you, babe. I love you and honor you.

Thank you to all three of my parents—Guy Wilson and Rob and Kelly Hallum—for supporting me through the entire process of writing this book, and for allowing me to share part of your story while telling mine. I could not ask for better parents. You have always believed in me, loved me, and prayed for me. I love you all so much!

Thank you to our prayer team (you all know who you are) for fervently praying this book into existence. It would not have happened without you all!

I want to give a special thank you to Jim Kochenburger for editing my book and Evan Leake for creating my cover. Also, to Tabbitha Mosier for the photography. You all made my book beautiful!

Most of all, thanks to God who saved me. You have my heart, voice, and life.

TABLE OF CONTENTS

FOREWORD

One of the great catalysts for a genuine change in life comes through encountering the passionate story of someone else's triumph over tragedy. Whether rags-to-riches or trauma-to-transformation, we are deeply influenced by hearing eyewitness accounts and personal witness testimonies.

When I accepted Heather's invitation to share with the girls in her sphere of influence, there were a few things I could have expected. I could have expected to see beautiful people who like worship music and powerful preaching, because Heather is a brilliant expression of all these things, however, I did not expect to observe the raw honesty, simple transparency, and bold passion that were evident as a bond among these girls. It was clear that Heather's story and love for Jesus had a far-reaching effect and great impact on them.

In my thirty plus years of ministering to others through missions and church planting, I have seen those who acknowledged their pain and need for change, but who had not experienced anything more powerful and compelling than the difficult moment in which they were trapped. That is, until one person's passionate portrayal of the grace of God in his or her life awakened hope and activated faith in their lives as well. Similarly, these girls who had seen Heather's life and heard her story shared a common kind of tipping point experience that profoundly changed them. Each carried a sense of relief that comes from being rescued from a painful past, intermingled with the responsibility to share life openly with anyone who might benefit. These women had experienced change and were out to change their world for Jesus.

As you read Heather's book, *Unscarred*, remember that this is her personal story, in her own words. You may experience a range of emotions just as I did. Of all the emotions you might experience, I hope you will be inspired to extend grace to those who are caught in the crevasses of life as Heather was.

I am sure you will be curious about the passion that has turned this wayward teenager into a passionate leader. I pray you will be encouraged to know the transforming power of Jesus the same way that Heather does.

Judith Crist
Cofounder, Senior Pastor
City of Grace

Judith serves beside her husband, Dr. Terry M. Crist, to build a church culture that reflects the vibrancy of heaven: sincere, loving relationships and inspiring environments where people are transformed. She is a student of God's Word and loves sharing her story of healing and grace.

PROLOGUE

My life had spiraled out of control and I was being forced to confront my own inner demons . . . but by whom? I was not sure. I did not have the self-control or desire to do it on my own. I could feel something coming but did not know what. I was nervous and filled with anxiety—extreme anxiety! I felt as if everyone and everything was so far away from me. I created distance from my friends and had not shared anything personal with my family in a long time. I felt completely isolated, but I could sense somehow that my life was drastically changing and about to change even more!

One weekend I planned to go up to visit my boyfriend, Jack, at his college, and take a couple of my friends along with me. We curled our hair, put on pounds of makeup, got all "dressed up," and headed north for a two-hour drive. When we arrived, Jack and one of his buddies, Rick, greeted us. The weekend was off to a good start when they pulled out their pipe and weed. We all sat in a circle in Jack's dorm room and he lit the pipe and passed it to one of my friends, who then passed it to Rick. Rick handed me the pipe and that's when it happened . . . somehow, my life was hijacked!

The whole room paused. When I say paused, I mean *paused!* Everyone was completely silent and looked frozen! It was as if someone had hit the pause button on a movie I had been watching. Everyone appeared frozen in mid-conversation and had awkward looks on their faces. However, this was no movie . . . this was real life . . . my life!

As you might imagine, I was in shock. Just then, I heard a voice speak to me, saying, "Is this what you *dreamed* of as a little girl? Did you dream of growing up to *live* this kind of life? Is this what you want your *purpose* to be in this world? Do you really *enjoy* this lifestyle? Is this everything you *imagined* your life to be?" I heard all these questions, though audibly or in my head, I am not sure. I heard them loud and clear and every hair on the back of my neck and arms stood up as goose bumps covered my arms and legs! One thing was sure; these were great questions and I had never thought about them before. After all, I was still young—seventeen! However, I felt thirty, as if I had already lived so much life for one so young (which was, I began thinking, maybe not such a good thing). I actually felt exhausted, drained, and in some weird way, as if I was being *awakened*. Then from beneath those questions, deep within me, I noticed a small soft voice rise, saying over and over, "No, no, no, no, no."

Suddenly, everyone snapped out of it, starting right off from where they had left off, that is, until I interrupted them, yelling, "No!"

"What do you mean, 'No?'" they asked before mocking me and suggesting I must have already been high. As they began laughing and shoving the pipe in my face, I felt an anger different from any I had ever felt before beginning to rise up in me. I was pissed that they would not listen to me and were mocking me for trying to do a good thing by refusing their weed. They were supposed to be my friends and hear me out! Quitting drugs was actually the right thing to do, so why were my friends not supporting me? I was not criticizing their decision, just hoping for support for mine. Though I was seated right there with them, I suddenly felt completely separate from them. Indignation and strength rose up in me.

"I quit! I'm done with this! No more!" I said in response to their ridicule before standing up and leaving the circle.

"You know you'll be right back here with us next weekend, doing the same thing, so you might as well come back over here," one of them said. "You seriously think you're just gonna quit after years of doing this? Come on, chill out and come smoke with us."

"I told you, I'm done! And I won't be back here next weekend doing this with you! I'll prove it to you!"

My competiveness had kicked in for a good cause and I could not wait to prove all of them wrong! My competiveness became my own accountability. I had no support system. I would not have known what to tell anyone anyway. Surely I was not going to tell my parents.

I had been a mess for years! I mean, I obviously had not planned to do this on my trip to see my boyfriend at college. Where had my newfound strength and desire to do the right thing come from? Was this just a pride thing? I could not tell. (Though had it been up to my pride to get me through quitting, I would have taken it!) I knew it was something else; I just could not put my finger on it. I had no explanation, I was just . . . *done*.

"My competiveness became my own accountability."

Returning home from that weekend, I was filled with so many new questions: *What just happened? Whose words were those? What is going on in my life? Who am I?*

CHAPTER 1
MA & POPS

I need to explain a small part of my parent's story to tell my whole story. The history of a thing brings revelation and understanding for present and future. I will start with my mom.

Mom was raised by parents who fell in love at a very young age—only fourteen years old! My grandma was pregnant with my mom at seventeen years of age and married the same year. My grandma was pregnant again two years later with my mom's only sibling, a brother. My grandparents were forced to grow up extremely fast, having the responsibility of children, bills, marriage, and all the rest.

My mom and her brother were brought up in a Christian home, but a different kind of Christian home. The church they were a part of was very religious (in an unhealthy way); more about laws than relationship, more about control than love. They taught false doctrine and not the true Word of God. For example, they taught that women were not allowed to cut their hair or wear make-up, which was weird. Though my grandparents later realized their church was actually more of a cult, until then it had a great effect on the way they lived and parented, which made for a difficult home life for my mom and her brother.

Being raised by extremely young parents heavy influenced by a cultish church established for my mom a home atmosphere ripe for rebellion. My mom had been taught that her only purpose was to be a wife and, after that, a mother. She was put on diets at the age of ten, taught to shave her legs, trained in the responsibilities of a wife, given many chores, and taken out of school to find a husband.

My mom was a smart child, so when she was taken out of school, she took quite a confidence hit. Because of being placed on diets as a child, she grew up with many insecurities. It had been humiliating for her to be trained as a prospective wife and mother as a young girl, before she was naturally ready. A little girl wants to play dress up and worry about little girl things. They are not built to carry grown-up roles and responsibilities. This type of upbringing, coupled with a church that condoned false prophecy, had no love, and controlled women, as I wrote earlier, was a setup for *rebellion!* At least it was for a strong-willed girl with a mind of her own, as my mom definitely was!

I need to pause here for a moment. You might be thinking, *Why did they raise a little girl that way?* It is important to understand that peoples' thought processes and ways are passed on for generations and generations. I will not take time to get into it, but my grandparents also did not have an easy background: one was raised by an alcoholic father, the other was raised by a sex offender! My grandparents did the best they knew how and tried to do the right thing by raising their children in church. However, like many young people, they were gullible, naive, and easily taken advantage of and manipulated. My grandparents, mom, and her brother were easy victims. This was a case of babies raising babies, and the bad influences surrounding them wore "good guy" masks. Because of all this, my mom was eager to escape. However, when she did reach out for freedom, she ran right into her first love's arms . . . my dad.

My dad was raised in a very abusive atmosphere. His father, was raised during the Great Depression, and was extremely greedy, had no faith in God, and was a womanizer and drinker who lacked love. He was a mean man, extremely selfish, and he cared more about money and possessions than any human or relationship. When my dad was only six years old, my granddad sat him down, opened up a beer for my dad and him, and said, "It's time for me to teach you how to be a man." He was six years old, drinking a beer, and being given a man talk by the one serving up the drinks? Obviously my granddad had a few screws loose!

My grandmother loved my father very much. Unfortunately, she found out she had cancer when he was only sixteen years old. This changed things a lot. My grandparents divorced and my granddad quickly found other women. My dad explained his childhood to me as being a harsh one with no real intimate father and son moments.

As my grandma's cancer progressed, my dad had to take care of her more and more. He had to watch her become incredibly sick due to chemo treatments, and lose her hair. She aged quickly as she fought a losing battle, which only further embittered my dad toward his own father. At one point during the battle, it seemed as if she was getting better. She even remarried! Everyone loved her new husband, Ron—especially my dad. Ron finally brought my dad the love and attention he needed. Ron made him feel like a real son. They had fun together, even going on father and son outings—things he had never done with his biological father.

Not long into their marriage, Ron was diagnosed with cancer. Even worse, it was in advanced stages and progressed so rapidly that within months, he was gone. My dad lost the first man he truly felt loved by, and was left with a selfish, mean father who cared little for him. He was then left with his mother and cared for her as she resumed her battle with cancer. It is no surprise that from a young age, he was tormented by pain, rejection, and generational curses.

Broken

My mom was seventeen and my dad was twenty-one when they met. My mom was gorgeous and caught my dad's eye right away. My dad was also good-looking and they looked "right" together—the perfect couple, it seemed.

My mom, naïve, due to her controlling, religious upbringing, fell completely in love with my dad, desiring the marriage and family she had been raised to believe was her only destiny. My dad, on the other hand, was eager to have his own life after enduring all the stresses of his life growing up and being pushed out on his own at such a young age. He was "overly experienced" and just wanted to party, have fun, have a hot girl by his side, drink, and experiment a little bit. When he met my mom, he was doing exactly that while dealing drugs. My mom, on the other hand, had been so sheltered she had never seen drugs, so she did not understand how deep into them he was. In their own ways, both were rebelling against their upbringing. This drove them right into each other's arms . . . and they brought every hurt and pain of the past with them. It was a recipe for disaster.

At nineteen years old, my mom found out she was pregnant with me. Due to pressure from my mom's parents, my mom and dad were married before I was born. My mom hoped this would slow my dad down and be exactly what he needed to help him become a good husband and father. But my dad did a good job hiding his drug dealing and drug use as he knew none of it would fly with my mom. However, he did not hide it all and his behavior remained unchanged. This caused a lot of friction in their marriage, to say the least. He was too deep in and did not understand that his upbringing had more power over him than making a promise to stop.

When I came along, my dad was still living the way he wanted to. My mom began to suspect he was messing around with other women, so the fighting between them escalated. My mom started catching my dad dealing and using drugs. She left him many times, taking me away to my grandparents for both of our safety. However, he would always call and tell her how much he truly loved us (especially me), how much he wanted us back, and promise he would change.

Unfortunately, dad had no clue how to change. The cycle was always the same. He would try to straighten out for a short time, but then get frustrated when he could not maintain the "family life." Then he would convince himself that he had a right to live as he had because he was young, citing all he had been through growing up. This cycle always brought him back into the world of partying, drugs, and girls.

By the time I was two years old, my dad had lost all control and respect for his own family. He quit hiding much of his wild lifestyle. It was no longer a choice, it was overtaking his entire being . . . it was becoming him. It did not help that his mother lost her battle with cancer. It was as if he had a new reason to fall deeper.

One day, my mom found me with some of dad's drug paraphernalia in my little hands that I had found. She had finally had enough. She packed up our stuff and moved us in with my grandparents.

A short time after this, my mom found out she was pregnant with my brother. At twenty-one years old, my mom had a two-year-old (me) and another child on the way. My mom and dad decided to try to make things work for the sake of the family, but things only escalated. Their hope for change was short-lived.

The stress on my mom was extreme due to being pregnant and having to worry about where her husband was, what he was doing, and with whom. During the third trimester of her pregnancy, they had an all-out fight. My dad got physically abusive with my mom and she had to go to the hospital to make sure everything was okay with the baby, my brother.

After my mom was discharged from the hospital, she returned home to find another woman moving into our house. This woman told my mom it was over for her and that her husband (my dad) was now her man and it was her house now. As you might imagine, my mom lost it — so much so that she considered suicide. She would later tell me that she would have killed herself had she not been carrying my brother inside her. (She says my brother saved her life.) I cannot imagine the pain she must have felt at that point, or the depths of the hopelessness she felt as she faced the end of her marriage to the father of her two children. She divorced my father and lived and worked as a single mother.

My parents were as broken as ever. My dad fully indulged in a life of drugs and women, as he had deceived himself into believing this was his right and the true desire of his life. He pushed away the family he had always desired as a kid and the family that loved him. Though my mom believed her solitary purpose in life was to find and wed a husband and raise a family with him, she was now left alone to raise her children on her own. She had been lied to, cheated on, abused and humiliated, and she now had to go on with life. Her life leads into my life.

CHAPTER 2

ME

Growing up, I remember being a pretty angry kid. My parents being divorced put early insecurities in me. Of all my friends, there were only a couple of us with divorced parents. It was not as common back then I did not understand why my parents were not together. I just wanted to feel "normal," but I could not escape feeling that I did not belong. Early in life I came to believe I had to be a fake "me" to be accepted.

One of the oddities of my life was I had two Christmases — Christmas Eve with my dad and Christmas morning with my mom. We had two separate "everythings" actually — two homes, two different bedrooms, two different lives. Things were completely different at my dad's house from my mom's house. Later on, I would meet some kids from divorced families who said they felt lucky to have two of everything, but that was not my reality. My parents did not get along. For me, it felt like we were always being shipped back and forth and fought over. We felt like paychecks with price tags on our foreheads.

I remember my dad telling me that my mom was stealing from him through child support. He said she was making him pay her money for us kids, but then pocketing it for herself. He would have my brother or I hand her the check most of the time. I felt sad and ashamed. I started questioning who my mom truly was, never questioning whether my dad was telling the truth. He was my dad and that was enough for me. How was I to know my dad was speaking out of years of pain and rejection, and that my mom was none of the things he claimed? I did not dare tell my mom he said these things.

However, my image of her began to be tainted. I was so confused. My dad may not have understood that minimizing his mistakes, making excuses, and even defending his behavior was polluting me. I was already confused enough, having no idea why my parents were not together. That was a big question in my mind. My mom was quiet about the reasoning (probably trying to protect us), but she was unaware of the steady stream of "answers" my dad was giving me—mostly portraying my mom as an evil person.

It did not help that two years after their divorce, when I was four, my mother remarried and I got a stepbrother. I felt as if my stepdad had stolen my mom from me—especially when I could no longer sleep with her as I always had. Awkward does not begin to describe how difficult it was for me as a little girl to wrap my mind around watching another man move in with my mom and start acting like my dad. I did not want another dad! I wanted *my* dad to be my dad with *my* mom! I felt as if this guy came in and ruined that. My mom, still in the middle of her healing process, did not realize I had not begun mine yet. They quickly got pregnant with my youngest brother. They had started their life together and I felt lost in between their lives—the life of my mom, my new stepdad, and my father.

"My mom, still in the middle of her healing process, did not realize I had not begun mine yet."

Rage

All of this generated a tremendous amount of anger within me as a little girl. I was afraid of the unknown in my life so I always responded in anger. I fought with my brother all the time. By fight I do not mean normal sibling fighting, I mean thirty-minute wrestling and all-out punching fights in the backyard. (My dad would let us duke it out for as long it took until one of us prevailed or could not take it anymore, which was usually my brother because I was older and bigger.) At times, I locked him in chests and left him there. I tied him to chairs with tape over his mouth a couple times. A few times, I left him in a dark bathroom tied up for hours until one of my parents came to his rescue. I was full of hatred and sadly, I took it out on my younger brother. The buried emotional pain in me kept building and started to boil over. Eventually, I was unable to hold it in.

My dad played the role of "cool dad," letting us do whatever we wanted whenever we wanted. When we were younger and visited my dad's house, we ate all the unhealthy things we wanted to, watched whatever we wanted to (every horror movie you could imagine), went to bed whenever we wanted to — all with no discipline.

My mom was the exact opposite and very structured. At her house, we always ate healthy, followed schedules (including set bedtimes), attended church, and had a lot of discipline. It is obvious which parent might be more appealing to a child, and our dad knew it. He wanted to be our favorite, so he would feel confident in his relationship with his kids. Vacations, gifts, and holidays all became a competition. My mom hated this, of course! She responded by being even stricter, believing this was necessary to undo the bad habits my dad was instilling in us every other weekend. This was underscored by our stepdad, who I did not like . . . at all! To him, everything had to be perfectly clean, our rooms had to be immaculate, beds had to be made the right way, the kitchen was closed at a certain time, and more. He was incredibly anal! OCD anal! All this made my mom and stepdad more and more unappealing to me as I compared their home life with the laid back, fun weekends with my dad.

There were things I did not look forward to at my dad's house. He had a number of different girlfriends who were in and out of our lives. I would always get attached to them and then never see them again. He never went long without a new one. My dad wanted to mirror the image of the put together family my mom had so badly that he said of every new girl he dated, "She might be your future stepmom." I would then totally fall in love with the new girlfriend . . . and then they would be gone — no goodbyes. As a result, I had this extreme up and down, roller coaster feeling about my life. I wanted consistency, but it was unattainable in our divorced family.

Attention, Attention, Attention

Neither of my parents understood what was going on in my little brain. Even I did not know what was going on up there. They were so busy overcompensating for what they believed to be the mistakes of the other that I was beginning to think I was the mistake. I was overly spoiled and overlooked all at the same time. I craved being the center of attention, and if I was not, I was jealous of whoever I perceived to be the center of attention, whether my brother, my stepdad, friends at school—anyone. I craved attention.

I remember visiting my cousins' house one time and being so jealous of them because they had a new Polly Pocket toy I wanted so badly. They had so little, but I wanted it . . . and wanted them to not have it! I was ashamed of how I felt because I loved them and got along great with them normally, but jealousy rose up in my little heart over this toy, so I quickly thought of an idea. I talked them into playing hide-and-seek, and when they hid, I took their Polly Pocket and put it in my bag. One of them caught me and said she had seen me take their toy. I lied to them, telling them I had not taken it. Later on that day, I went home.

The next day, my aunt called my mom and stepdad to tell them about the toy, that it was missing, and that their girls thought I had taken it. My mom asked me about it, but I tried to lie again. My mom saw right through me! I felt so embarrassed and ashamed! If that was not enough, my mom made me personally bring back the toy, tell the truth, and apologize (rightfully so!). I was humiliated. That was not the kind of attention I craved!

If I did not get the attention I wanted, I did not feel loved (though this was a false sense of love). The generational curse of rejection had been passed on to me.

"If I did not get the attention I wanted, I did not feel loved (though this was a false sense of love)."

When I was eight years old my dad married a woman named Sandy. My brother and I really liked her when they were dating. She had given my brother all her old Army clothes from her time in the military, and given me some '80s dress-up clothes. She had no children, so we would be her first. My dad thought she was the one who would complete our family. He told us to call her "Mom," but it felt weird. She did not feel like a mom. This was another big change in my life about which I had no say and no understanding.

I'll never forget when our dad told my brother and I that we would be in their wedding. We were so excited about that! It made it feel somewhat right. I could not wait to be my dad's flower girl! However, right before the wedding our dad told us Sandy had made the decision that no kids were allowed. The wedding was going to be small, with only them, close friends, and family. I was heartbroken! The one thing that had me excited about the whole thing was getting to be a part of that day. It would be a time to be a family and bond with Sandy as my new mom. I could not understand why she made the decision she did not want us there. How was I supposed to take that? This triggered another feeling of incredible rejection within me! Again, I was not asked how I felt about it; my dad just told me and left.

When my dad and Sandy returned from their honeymoon, she was a different woman! She came back militant — the anti-mom. She hated my brother and I. She felt we were the things standing between her and my dad's true happiness. She figured that after the wedding, my dad would become so committed to her that he would leave us and move away so they could start their own life together.

She was awful to us. She screamed and yelled at us. She locked us in our rooms for most of the day when my dad was not at home. She always embarrassed us in front of our friends. There was not a nurturing bone in the woman's body!

I remember one morning, Sandy and my dad took us out for breakfast. I ordered the traditional breakfast: eggs, toast, and sausage. I ate the eggs and toast but left the sausage because I did not like sausage. (I truly did not eat any kind of pork and still do not to this day.) She took the opportunity to torture me over the dumb uneaten sausage.

"We aren't leaving this restaurant until you finish your entire meal! You ordered it, you eat it!" Sandy screamed at me.

"But I don't like pork. I don't want to eat it!" I said.

"You are going to do what I tell you! You will eat that sausage!"

We argued for a few minutes until I was in tears. Finally, my dad stepped in and said I did not have to eat it right then. Sandy asked the waitress for a box so we could take the sausage home. She warned me that before I ate anything else, I was to eat that sausage. We left for home. A few hours later, it was lunchtime. I went into the kitchen and started making myself a sandwich. Just then, I heard the master bedroom door fly open and there was Sandy, screaming at me and asking, "What do you think you're doing?"

"I'm hungry and I'm just making a sandwich for lunch," I said.

She ripped everything out of my hands, threw it away, and put the rest in the fridge. Then she pulled out the box of sausage from earlier that morning and shoved it in my face.

"You're going to eat this before you touch any other food!" she shouted. "I don't care if you starve for days—you're going to eat this sausage!"

I started crying and ran to my room and shut the door. I stayed there until my dad got home from work late that night. I cried all day and wrote in my diary about how much I hated my new mom. I told my dad about what she had done. I told him that I did not want to visit him at his house when she was there.

My dad started to see how she treated us. He also could not get over the discussions she was having with him about leaving us with our mom so the two of them could take off and start their own lives together. Unknowingly, she made a big mistake: She underestimated the love our dad had for us. My granddad had been such a mean and unloving father to my dad that my dad had set his mind on loving us no matter what, and there was no way he was going to leave us. He told Sandy this, which did not go over well. By the end of their first year of marriage, they were divorced.

At my mom's house, I was struggling with the same kind of hatred toward my stepdad. I remember one of the first times my mom had him over to our house. I was four years old at the time. They were sitting on the couch and he had his arm around my mom. I remember being very angry over this. I went over to them and squished myself between them and took his arm off my mom. He could have been the best guy in the world, but it did not matter to me. I was not ready for all of that change. I had always been my mom's little shadow. I followed her everywhere, slept with her every night, and wanted to look like her and be like her. After they married, when I was five, I remember having a talk with my mom about my stepdad and my need for more of her (at least I tried to express that). She tried to explain to me that she was supposed to put her husband first.

"Not before me!" I responded angrily.

"Honey, my husband is supposed to come first, and then you kids."

I was totally crushed! I did not understand all that marriage stuff and who was to be first or whatever—I was five! I just wanted more of my mom. I was having a hard time with all of the changes and did not know how to say it. Her response was the last thing I needed to hear. It embittered my heart toward my new stepdad. I wanted nothing to do with a man who came in and took my mom from me, but I was stuck with him. I decided that I would hate him, not listen to him, and run more to my dad. It all seemed to be one big, bad setup: the abandonment I felt; the things my dad told me about my mom; bringing new "parents" into my life; my mom allowing the new "dad" to take my place and hearing her actually say that he had to be her number one, not me. It had to have been a setup!

Deeper and deeper I buried my painful emotions and hurt. Like stepping in gum, I felt trapped within an overwhelming sense of rejection. The more I tried to get it off me the more it stuck to me! I developed major insecurities, competitiveness, and jealousy at a young age. I felt an unhealthy pressure come on me to be perfect. Perfection, I thought, would please others and me. However, I couldn't handle all the pressure, pain, and hurt, so I continued to act out in anger.

"Perfection, I thought, would please others and me."

At about thirteen years of age I started to really show disrespect to my parents. A scary boldness came upon me, driven by tremendous rage. Little did I know, this unhealthy combination was about to thrust me into a destructive downward spiral.

CHAPTER 3
MY EARLY TEENS

This is when *everything* began with me. I was a straight A student and played volleyball, basketball, and softball. I took school very seriously, and so did my parents. I remember being so afraid of disappointing my mom and stepdad on my grades that I would do anything to keep them up. On the other hand, I wanted to make my dad proud by being a good athlete. He coached a lot of my brother's and my teams growing up. Sports were a big deal to my dad. I was trying so hard to keep up a positive image with my family, teachers, coaches, and everyone else, that I started to overwhelm myself. My perfectionistic personality can make me my own worst enemy at times—especially back then. I wanted to be loved by everyone and be the popular girl everyone else wanted to be.

The sad thing was, I was pretty much that girl. I hated myself so much that I could not see it. I had girls trying to be like me while I was trying to be like them!

As if being a teenager was not hard enough, with all of my issues, it was nearly impossible.

I started spending more time at my dad's and friends' houses because I had much more freedom at those places. I started meeting new people—older people. Many of my friends had older siblings, and their older siblings had older friends, so hanging out with them felt cool.

When I was fourteen years old I met a senior in high school, Tim. He was eighteen, had a fast car and total freedom, and I thought he was *so* cool! He drove me around, took me to Seattle, took me racing with him—it was all a total adrenaline rush. I took my first drinks of alcohol and smoked my first cigarettes with Tim.

Tim saw me as a fearless, young, pretty girl and brought me my first bit of freedom and excitement. I did not see the beauty in me. My insecurity veil had blinded me from seeing any kind of beauty or value in myself. However, what I could not see, Tim and others did see. Knowing Tim and others were attracted to me made me feel good about myself, wanted, and loved.

"My insecurity veil had blinded me from seeing any kind of beauty or value in myself."

Sidenote: It is scary for young girls when the attention they get is typically not the kind they want, or comes from those whose motives are not pure. There are many out there who desire to take from us and leave us in broken pieces. They see flesh and want flesh. You may see them and think, *Prince Charming*, when the only things charming about them are their clever one-liners and suave half smiles. *Confidence* is rare in this generation of young girls, and many girls who do have it base it on fleshly things. Confidence needs to make a comeback in this generation of young girls and women—confidence based on *purpose and destiny*, not how big your boobs are or how skinny you are.

Guys, you need to try looking for something deeper than *flesh* and you may find what you are really looking for: a teammate who will have your back and support you in all you want to do. If you realize a girl is trying to catch you with her body, remember, it will not be long until she rushes right over to the next guy who gives her attention. You will not cure the insecurity in her, and she will not cure your lust! Bottom line: *Look deeper.*

My dad overlooked my relationship with Tim, but my mom knew nothing about it because I kept it hidden from her. It was part of the life I lived only when I was at my dad's or friends' houses.

Tim was also my first sexual experience. He wanted to have sex, but I was afraid so I told him no. Still, he persisted in pushing himself on me to do sexual things. I had guts enough to stop things from going too far, but I still was always left feeling ashamed and embarrassed.

"Confidence needs to make a comeback in this generation of young girls and women — confidence based on *purpose and destiny*, not how big your boobs are or how skinny you are."

Up to that point I had only kissed one other person, on a dare, and hated it! I did it and walked away from the boy. I had a couple boyfriends in middle school, but these were more drama things than relationships. I was not allowed to talk to boys at my mom's house. (I was actually glad about this because I did not want to!) I only said yes to the guys who asked me out because I enjoyed the attention (and did not know how to tell them no). Plus, my best friends and I had a competition to see who could date the most guys. I did not talk on the phone with these boys, go on dates with them, or kiss them. I did not even allow them to walk me to my class. For me, the idea was fun, but not so much actually following through to "real dating."

While trying to be something I was not, I went from a kiss on a dare to my first sexual experience at fourteen with an eighteen-year-old guy! I did not want that! I wanted the romance and friendship, but not the sexual part. Obviously, he wanted the opposite.

I was so embarrassed by it all that I slowly tried not talking to him anymore. However, something about that merely numbed me. It was as if I said in my heart, *Well, now that that happened, there is not much left*. I remember feeling less of a person than before . . . and becoming more careless.

Sidenote: Any time you try to be someone you are not designed to be, *you will fail . . . miserably*! You are called to live out your purpose, not someone else's. You were designed to do what *only you* can do, while others were designed to do what only they can do. So, if you are trying to do what only others can do, how can you succeed? What you were made to do will never be accomplished if you do not live out what you were called to do! *You* are the best *you*! Be confident in you and stop looking to others for how to act, dress, or talk unless the person is trustworthy, like a parent, teacher, or someone who has given you good counsel in life, who can see in you what you cannot see in you! This individual must be a good influence who has pure motives for speaking into your life. Sometimes it takes the pure-hearted leadership of another to pull out of us what we do not see in ourselves. Though we all have convictions about what we should and should not do, we must *listen* to those convictions and not ignore them.

"Any time you try to be someone you are not designed to be, *you will fail . . . miserably!*"

Identity Crisis

My home life felt so messed up. Its foundation was so shaky that it made me feel as if I might fall through the cracks at any moment! I actually had nightmares of trying not to fall through the cracks of a canyon that was breaking up beneath me and all around me. I would slip through one of the cracks but then barely catch myself on a ledge before falling into the darkness. Everything would continue to shake—the ground, the ledges I had barely caught—and I would fall again before awakening with a jolt, sweating, happy it was only a dream. I had the feeling my reoccurring dream had something to do with what I was going through.

I had built walls around my life to keep certain people out, but it was as if everyone could see right through them. Like all my parent's mistakes and all of my mistakes were filmed and being viewed by all. I felt as if my life was a reality show and when I showed up the next day at school, I wondered who had seen all my embarrassing moments. My mom and I fought all the time. It got physical a couple times. I hated her. I hated her for marrying my stepdad and choosing him over me. I hated her for never standing up for me when I got in arguments with my stepdad. I hated her for all the things my dad told me about her. I simply hated her, but even more so, my stepdad. They grounded me for everything, it seemed. I felt smothered and controlled, with no freedom. This was only made worse by the total freedom I enjoyed while staying with my dad, where I came and went whenever I wanted to, and went wherever I wanted to go. In comparison to no boundaries at all, my mom and stepdad were suffocating! I felt no love from them, only harshness and discipline.

I was fourteen years old and living two separate lives. I clung to my friends. With friends, I was the happy, funny daredevil. Many of my friends would roll their eyes at me and try to stop me from playing stupid pranks, doing crazy things like jumping off bridges into rivers, or getting into fights. I did not play pranks to be cute; I was trying to shock people. It was all a show I would put on to get their attention. I remember one of those times . . . vividly.

One night I slept over at the home of Hannah, a friend of mine since childhood, along with another close friend, Ashley. Ashley and I always got into trouble together. While Hannah was in the shower, we decided we wanted to freak her out. So Ashley and I decided to go out to her garage to see if we could come up with something. The garage door was open, so we walked up her driveway to the road. We noticed a huge dead animal on the side of the road. Ashley and I both started laughing obnoxiously and began planning our prank! I ran back to the garage and grabbed her dad's shovel. I scraped the huge animal off the pavement and my partner in crime helped me carry it to Hannah's room. We laughed hysterically the whole way, never thinking of how upset she might be . . . was *surely* going to be. I do not think we cared!

I pulled back the covers and Ashley and I placed the roadkill right in the middle of her bed. Then we pulled the sheets and comforter up to cover it. We ran the shovel back to the garage to cover up the evidence. Just as we got back to the room we heard Hannah get out of the shower. We ran down to the living room to watch TV and pretend we were being good (as if the dead animal crawled into her bed by itself). We heard her walk out of the bathroom and both began silently laughing with excitement, anticipating her response. Suddenly we heard a bloodcurdling scream! Then Hannah angrily shouted my name. I just laughed uncontrollably. She ran down to where we were, crying hysterically and screaming at me to leave and never come back. I tried to calm her down but nothing worked. I packed my bags and went home. I did not return to her house until sometime later, when my mom found out and made me bring her flowers and apologize. Hannah kept me at a distance from then on (rightfully so).

I was truly friends with just about everybody; the good kids and the bad kids, the older kids and the younger kids. In fact, my social life was my whole life! It was the most important thing in the world to me. My parents started getting concerned because I would stay a couple nights with my friends without returning home. I had fallen in love with my new identity and the love of my friends.

Movin' Out, Movin' In

When I was fifteen years old, I made the decision to move in with my dad so I could concentrate on what was important to me—my social life. At my mom's, it was about grades, structure, church, and manners. My dad did not care about much of that at the time. He merely wanted me to try my best in school, do well in athletics, and have fun being a teenager. He allowed me to run my own life as long as it did not disrupt his. He let me make all my own decisions as long as I kept a job, so I did. That gave me money for whatever I wanted to do anyway. I was also a very convincing liar. I knew how to talk my way out of anything and how to convince my dad (especially) to trust me with everything. I partnered lies with manipulation and the combination became my game.

I moved in with my dad during my freshman year of high school. My mom could not fight me anymore—I made her and my stepdad miserable! Plus, they still had my three younger brothers to raise. I know she hoped I would see that the grass was not greener on the other side, but she did not know the things I had my mind set on. She had no clue about the things I had already done and wanted to do more of.

My dad had a big alcohol cabinet from which I would regularly partake whenever I wanted to. He never said anything about the missing bottles to me. He never asked questions about where I went or with whom. My dad had a big shop with living space inside, and I threw a few parties there at night, for friends right after moving in. My dad was in bed by seven because he had to get up at three in the morning for work, so it was perfect. Our house and the shop were in the middle of nowhere, with no authority figures around. Everybody started talking about "my place" and I started throwing more and more parties there.

At the time, my mind raced with excitement over finally being able to get away with the stuff I wanted to get away with and be who I wanted to be. No one was jumping down my throat, interrogating me, or grounding me anymore.

A close friend of mine happened to live just a mile down the road from me and she always had parties and invited older guys. I began thinking that maybe the whole sexual experience I had was not such a bad thing. The embarrassment had faded by that time, and I began to think the experience actually made me more mature. I was not beating myself up about it, but I also was not going around blabbing about it to everyone (Tim had already taken care of that). In fact, I started to think the "experience" could make me more confident. After all, my older friends had done those things with their boyfriends, and I was like them now: older, more experienced, and someone who had proven she could hang with the older crowd.

This was the awful start to the growth of my false confidence.

CHAPTER 4

HIGH SCHOOL

False confidence is a dangerous thing, I have learned. You feel you have a reason to do whatever you want with boldness, when in reality your false confidence is a cover for big insecurities. The one who always seems to need to be the center of attention, who is most boisterous, happy, and seemingly has no concern what anyone else thinks, is often the one who cares most about what everyone thinks of him or her.

If you are truly confident, it comes from a place of peace within you. It is not made up, it is genuine. Confident people do not need to tell anyone they are confident. Confident people have no need to declare they do not care what others think of them. In fact, confident people care only what the *right* people have to say about them, and *receive* what they say with the sincere intention of improving themselves. Confident people do not care what the majority of people have to say, but not due to a rebellious mindset, but rather a respectful one. They know who they are, but are humble in this knowledge. This was not me. I was the false confident kind of person.

"Confident people do not need to tell anyone they are confident."

After moving in with my dad, I tried to spend as much time away from my mom's house as possible. I was all-in now.

Early in my freshman year, I met my first real boyfriend, Jack, a sophomore. He noticed me and came after me. After I had already fallen for him, I realized he had previously been a boyfriend of one of my friends (also a sophomore). This did not put me in a very good light with the older girls. I had known many of these girls since middle school (though I knew more of the older guys). I actually felt safer in high school with a boyfriend because I was "taken." I fell hard for Jack. He was an amazing athlete, got good grades, was good looking, and seemed like a great guy. I started spending most of my time with him.

Before long, I had sex for the first time, losing my virginity. I was fifteen years old. It happened one day when my dad was not home. I felt a sense of pressure that I had to act "grown-up" and be a "good girlfriend" — I am not quite sure why. But I felt I had to prove that I could have an older boyfriend. My heart did not want to do it, but the image of false confidence I had created wanted to go through with it, so we had sex.

The first time was definitely nothing special or romantic — nothing like I had imagined it would be. It was a big letdown really, except that afterward, I thought I might be more accepted. However, as it turned out, the only reason people really cared about it was to gossip.

That day opened up a whole new can of worms in my relationship with Jack. We had fooled around before in different ways, and I had never felt good about it, but after we had sex all I felt was deep pain. I felt disappointed with myself, though I did not recognize this at the time. From that day on, he definitely expected sex whenever he wanted it. He wanted to do things I did not want to do, and I felt like another piece of me had to be hidden. I felt so ashamed. I remember being mortified at even the thought of my parents finding out! People did not seem to like me more, in fact, except for my close friends, girls seemed to hate me more. Guys suddenly began making nasty comments to me that made me feel very uncomfortable. I expected none of this. For sure, this was nothing like the fairy tale girls dream about when they meet "the one"!

My heart had melted for Jack. Why? It might be because he was my first real boyfriend and high school sweetheart. Perhaps I wanted to feel grown up and dreamed of having a family like my mom had. I had long assumed that when I went "all the way," I had to give my whole heart, so I was not going to do that with just anybody. For some reason, that was the only moral thing that seemed to stick with me from all the church my mom brought me to as a kid, and all the talks I had with my grandparents while growing up. It might not have had so much to do with morals. It was not as if I was living any kind of a moral life. It just could have had to do with loyalty. I figured that because I gave him that part of me, I should expect a mature relationship in return, with trust and a future. Obviously, I was wrong about that. I was also too young to make decisions on things like who I would marry — I was only fifteen!

Diggin'

I quickly realized my expectations were far-fetched. It did not take long for him to cheat on me. I was devastated. My heart was broken and once again, I was humiliated. All the anger I had buried from my childhood rose back up in me. I could not hold it in anymore. It was boiling up and overflowing.

Though I already drank a lot of alcohol and smoked a lot of weed at the time, after Jack cheated on me, my partying with friends went to another level. I turned to alcohol and drugs as a coping mechanism to numb my pain. Smoking weed soon gave way to taking mild pain-killers and other pills. I started taking OxyContin, ecstasy, and finally, snorting cocaine. I experimented with all different kinds of drugs, but mainly stuck with cocaine and ecstasy. When I did not feel the high was strong enough, I started mixing large amounts of alcohol with drugs or simply doing more and more drugs, whatever it took.

I was an alcoholic before the age of sixteen. By the end of my sophomore year, I was doing drugs on a consistent basis. Every day I put some kind of drug in my body — whatever I had on hand.

I was still dating my boyfriend, Jack. In fact, I had taken him back many times over because I lacked the strength to fully break it off with him. To add insult to injury, he cheated on me not just with girls I did not know, but with some of my best friends, and even one of my cousins. I was so broken. I was full of hatred. I did not know who

I could trust. I had been humiliated so many times, I transferred my obsession from him to drugs and alcohol.

I started skipping a lot of school, but maintained good grades in spite of it, so my parents would not find out what I had been doing. I lost a lot of weight—I was pencil thin. I worked at a gym and was personal trained at 5 a.m. five days a week. After school, I went to practice for whatever sport I was playing at the time. Most evenings I would go on a three to five-mile run. I was working out 24/7. Due to all that exercise and the drugs and alcohol I used each day that ruined my appetite, I weighed in at 105 lbs. on my five feet eight inch frame. I had always been very muscular and thin, but every ounce of fat and muscle was gone at that point. I quit having my period and my mom began freaking out over my weight. The pressure was almost unbearable. I thought something was wrong with me since my boyfriend wanted other girls. I did not realize he had his own issues and that his mistakes did not have to reflect who I was. As skinny as I was, and considering the massive amount of drugs and alcohol I was consuming, I was putting my life at risk. However, I did not care. The only way I knew to alleviate the pressure and pain from the huge insecurity dose my boyfriend had given me (on top of all that was already there) was to take more drugs—more cocaine, pills, and alcohol.

At the time, I was friends with many different dealers and rich kids who could buy as many drugs as they wanted. Being a girl, I never had to worry about having money for drugs—they were given to me. My guy friends "took care of me." I grew up in a well-off little town built around a lake, with a lot of kids whose parents traveled frequently, leaving them large amounts of money on the counter to do with whatever they wanted while they were gone. And that is just what we did—whatever we wanted.

As a result, I found myself in some of the scariest and most disgusting places you can imagine. I will never forget the first time some friends and I visited one crack house we went to every once in a while to buy cocaine. It looked like a scene out of a horror movie! No electricity, running water, or heat . . . and we were in the Seattle area, which is cold! That house was the coldest house I had ever been in. People were lying all around, strung out. It seemed like there was no color inside the house, just a black and white scene. I remember checking out the house with one of my friends, just for shock value. In the upstairs bathroom we saw broken needles, blood, and syringes everywhere. The tub was full of batteries and acid. I was freaked out, but in spite of this, we still went back downstairs and snorted some cocaine with one of the few people still conscious. Then we left, as always, with our own rock of cocaine. We would drive just down the road, park, and snort more cocaine. Sometimes we ate shrooms and took pills while downing Jagermeister. Other times we would go find the cheapest motel we could, buy all the drugs we had money for, and have a drug sleepover, mixing things all night, trying to get as "gone" as possible.

One night I remember texting Jack to come and get me because I felt like I was about to die. (I never hung out with my boyfriend and my drug friends together. I never mixed the two.) The only thing I really remember was lying in a bathtub, fully dressed, but not knowing where I was or who I was with, and being unable to move very much. Whether I was just tripping or overdosing, I do not know, but I did not remember anything the next morning. Jack told me he had to carry me down the stairs and into the car and watch me all night to make sure I was okay. I do not know if he knew how scared I was or how much I had really done, but I knew what I was doing was a true cry for help. It felt good to have him come get me and help me. As sad as it sounds, I wanted to feel he loved me — that someone loved me. I felt crazy because my need for attention wanted someone to stop me from everything I was doing, but it also was the thing that lead me to get worse and worse. I had no boundaries, so even this situation and similar ones did not stop me. They did not even slow me down.

"I felt crazy because my need for attention wanted someone to stop me from everything I was doing, but it also was the thing that lead me to get worse and worse."

Can Anyone Hear Me?

I was the girl at the table with the guys in the early morning hours, still taking shots with them after all my girlfriends had been passed out for hours. Something had to have been protecting me back then, because the amount of drugs and alcohol I consumed for my body size should have killed me. Considering some of the places I went to, it was a miracle I made it out alive and unharmed. I knew there was something protecting me at other times too.

One night I was at a friend's house. She had an older sister with older guy friends. We had all been drinking and hanging out. I got tired and wanted to go to bed. The next thing I know, one of the older guys came in and shut and locked the door behind him. When I heard the lock, I was stricken with fear instantly. I knew something was wrong. He came over to the bed, pulled the covers right off me and got in bed with me. He tried to kiss me, but I turned my head and pushed him away. When I pushed him, he forced his weight on me. He was on top of me trying to take my clothes off, saying, "Shh." I told him no over and over, and tried to hold onto my clothes so he could not get them off me. He tried harder and harder, but I kept kicking him off me and yelling for my friend. Unfortunately, the house I was in was huge so she could not hear me. He tried kissing me again, thinking it would relax me, but I pushed his head away. I grabbed hold of the blanket and pulled it back over me, pushing him hard and cursing at him to get out, hoping to intimidate him. He started laughing at me in a mocking way and walked out. I started crying.

My friend eventually came to bed and I told her what had happened. She seemed more jealous than worried for me because she had liked him. No true friend would have responded that way. I was hurt by what had happened, but even more hurt by her response. I never told anyone about this after that. I did not want her blaming any part of it on me. I had been lied about and gossiped about before, so I did not want this getting out and being turned on me. I feared what Jack might have thought if he heard about it, so I stayed quiet.

The nightmare revisited me during my junior year. I was at a party one night with a different group of friends. These friends were "good kids." They were great athletes, got great grades, and came from good families. We were mainly just hanging out and celebrating our older friends' high school graduation, but drinking a little as well. One guy named Lee, my friend Alisha's boyfriend (and a good friend of my boyfriend, Jack), got obnoxiously drunk. (Jack did not come because we got into a big fight right before the party.) When we all went to bed, Alisha slept in a bed upstairs, but I slept in the bed in the master bedroom by myself.

Just as I was about to fall asleep, I heard the door crack open. It was Lee. He came in, jumped into bed with me, and started confessing feelings he had supposedly had for me for years. He begged me to be with him. He must have thought his drunken, slurred love confession and bad breath would cause me to swoon. All I could think about was how to escape. He leaned in for a kiss and I turned away and told him no. My refusal made him angry and he threw himself on me, trying to remove my clothes and attempting to kiss me all over. I kept kicking and pushing him off me, trying to remind him he was drunk and not in his right mind, but he would not stop pursuing. Then I tried reminding him of Alisha upstairs and anything else I could think of to get him to stop. Finally he paused, started crying and said he was sorry. I started to feel bad for him, so I told him I knew he was not like that and that he was just drunk and needed to go upstairs to bed. Instead, he jumped back on top of me, once again trying to get my clothes off me! It was like two different people inside of one body. I finally started yelling, which freaked him out, so he ran for the door. He came back in for a moment and pleaded with me not to say anything to anyone. Then he ran back out.

I was scared but also very pissed off. I called Jack to come pick me up. He picked me up and I started bawling. I wanted him to make me feel better and fix what happened, but he only seemed to be mad that his friend had tried something with his girlfriend—a puffed up pride/ego thing. I wanted him to be concerned for me and care about what I had just gone through, but I did not get that. We were silent the whole way home. I wondered if he was thinking it was my fault. Then I hoped no one would find out . . . again.

Deepest Regrets

By the time I was a junior in high school, I was as deep in as I was going to get. I went clubbing drunk and high every weekend, and regularly rode home with people I had just met. It would have been so easy for any random stranger to take advantage of me. Everything that had happened to me, instead of causing me fear or timidity, only created more recklessness in me. I felt like, *I've made it through all of that; I can make it through anything . . . I am invincible!*

One night opened my eyes to just how deep in I was. My best girlfriend, Danielle, and I had gone to a party out in the "boondocks." Many of our close friends were there, but there were also many people there we did not know, and the owner of the house was older. He had quite a few of his older buddies there, including a number of druggies and dealers. Half of the guys were total hicks — crazy, mindless hicks at that — and the other half were dealers with agendas. It was weird how they all came together at one place, but that is what drugs will do.

We were all drinking and dancing, thinking we were having a good time. Then one of the older guys made a pass at me. I responded with a smart-ass comment along the lines of, "Pa-lease . . . . You wish!" complete with a sarcastic roll of my eyes. He turned around quickly, grabbed me by the neck, and threw me up against a wall. He pushed me up against the wall, his hand still around my neck, until my feet were a foot off the ground, toes dangling, and yelled threats at me. One of my good guy friends, Jared, came over and punched him in the face, causing him to drop me. I fell to the floor grabbing my throat, trying to catch my breath. I looked up and saw the two of them fighting — blood everywhere. I yelled at other people to stop the fight as I watched my friend defending me. After Jared got the last hit in, some guys broke up the fight. I had no clue who or what I was dealing with that night. Most people would have left at that point . . . but that was just the beginning.

I stayed close to Jared all night, especially since many of my girlfriends had passed out or gone home. It was really late and I was very drunk. After hours of drinking games with the guys, I realized I had not seen Danielle in a while, so I went looking for her. I walked around asking anyone still awake if they had seen her. No one said they had seen her. I searched the entire bottom floor of the house and all around the outside of the house. She was nowhere to be found. I tried calling her cell, thinking maybe she had gone home with someone else and left her car because she had gotten too drunk. (Unfortunately, we all drove even when we were high or drunk. The only way we would not get behind the wheel was if it was impossible for us to climb behind the wheel.) She did not answer her phone.

There was one last place for me to check – the upstairs of the house they had closed off so no one would go up there into their bedrooms. I walked into one of the rooms and there was Danielle, lying on the bed passed out, her jeans around her ankles and blood all over the sheets and her legs. Three guys ran out of the room as I opened the door. As they brushed by my shoulder and ran down the stairs it hit me that the three of them had raped her. I woke her up and she told me she had to puke, so I carried her to the bathroom where she vomited over and over. Then she sat on the toilet to pee and realized she was in an immense amount of pain. She said it hurt too bad to go. I asked her what happened and she told me she had kissed one of the guys and the next thing she knew, he was forcing himself on her and calling his buddies in. She had been a virgin before this, and was sixteen years old (a year younger than me). I helped her get dressed and called Jared up to help me carry her down the stairs and out to the car. It hurt her too bad to walk by herself. We did not tell Jared what had happened because she did not want anyone to know. I had to take her to the doctor the next day. It was an awful time and now a horrible memory. That night changed her. It changed me too.

We never told anyone. Why? I do not know. I really have no answer for why we never told anyone or why the doctors did not do anything in the way of encouraging Danielle to tell someone. Maybe they did and we just did not listen due to the terror of the situation. I really do not know. It was as if we were in a trance and just rolled with whatever punches came our way. Before being raped, Danielle had never had sex or done any hard drugs. After it all happened, she turned into a different person – a young woman with no standards or self-confidence. She would have sex with anyone and do any kind of drug. She lost herself. She did not care about anything anymore. She went from someone under my bad influence to someone even more wild and careless than I was.

That was a night I will never forget – a night I wish I could take back and redo. To this day, Danielle is addicted to OxyContin and later dated and had a baby with one of the guys who raped her that night. I always felt guilt that I did not keep her by me and protect her. She was like my little sister, and I felt I failed her.

This became the first time I started to sense real right and wrong. We had done everything. We stole everything everywhere we went. We would eat at restaurants and leave without paying the bill. We would fill up our gas tank and drive off, steal groceries and beer, and more. Anything we could get our hands on, we took! I even taught her how to drive a stick shift in my car while smoking pot! I never felt real guilt . . . but that night Danielle was raped, I did.

Help!

Around this time, I attempted suicide twice—once at my mom's house and once at my dad's house. Each time, I had emptied my parents' cabinets and swallowed bottles of pills. I sat there waiting in fear to see what would happen to me.

I forget what triggered these attempts, but I know that overall, I was unhappy with my life without knowing why. I hated myself. If only I could be anyone else! I felt ugly though others said I was beautiful. I felt fat despite everyone saying I was too skinny. I felt unwanted though my parents fought over me. I felt angry but pretended to be full of joy. I felt depressed even when I was the comedian. I was full of hatred, though I was friends with everyone. Ultimately, I felt I was a failure. Was I? What was I trying to accomplish or be? What was this extreme pressure I put on myself that I felt I could not live up to? It did not make sense, but the pressure was there and I wanted to end it. I remember crying hysterically both times. And both times, I vomited excessively. I remember throwing up violently for hours each time, trying to cry between each urge. My body just threw it all up: No 9-1-1, no unconsciousness, and no one knew about either attempt. Somehow I was still alive. Something was protecting me. I went on with the life I hated . . . convinced I wanted it!

"Something was protecting me."

Throughout all of this, I worked at a local gym. I had known my boss, Mark, for years prior to working for him. He had been the kickboxing instructor for my mom and I for a few years before he decided to open his own gym. I started working for him from the start, even helping him open it.

Early on at the gym, my mom had pointed out to me a cute guy working out there. He wore a bandana around his head, a white tank top, and white basketball shorts. I told my mom to stop it because she knew I was still dating Jack. She did not care; my whole family hated him for all he had put me through. I ignored her matchmaking efforts.

Soon after, Mark started getting weird with me, bringing me small gifts and things at work, offering to do personal training sessions with me all the time, and asking me out. I really thought nothing of it because to me, he was old. (I was seventeen and he was in his mid-thirties.) I just thought it was great to have favor with my boss and for him to be able to trust me working for him . . . how naïve I was!

One night, I agreed to go to a Mariners game with him and two coworkers. As we drove into the gym parking lot that evening a limo was parked there. Mark's friend, Lance, and a girl named Julie were there as well. It felt a little awkward because it seemed as though it was an arranged double date and both guys were in their thirties and both of us girls were in our teens. I went along with it because I was excited about the baseball game.

When I got in the limo, there were drinks and beer so we started drinking on the way down to Seattle. When we arrived at the stadium, before we headed to our seats, Mark sent Lance to go buy us more drinks. Throughout the game, as soon as we finished our drinks, Lance would run up to get more. Before the seventh inning stretch, Mark was drunk and trying to put his arm around me. I felt super uncomfortable, so I did anything I could to politely let him know I was not okay with that kind of relationship with him. I would get up, go to the bathroom, or reposition myself, but he kept trying. I noticed that Lance and Julie were talking quietly and flirting a bit, so I began feeling more and more out of place. I decided I had enough to drink and was not going to drink any more.

The game ended and we got back in the limo and headed home. Only five minutes into our return trip home, he had the driver pull over at a gas station. He came out with a six-pack of beer! None of us needed anymore! He handed Julie and I beers and told us to chug. I immediately felt as if he was setting me up. I said, "No thank you," but he insisted. I sipped on it. He watched me the whole way home, asking over and over if I was done yet and ready for another one.

"I'm done drinking," I said again.

When we arrived back at the gym, he said he had to close down inside. So we all went in and Lance and Julie stepped off to the side to talk.

"Heather, can you come help me close down inside, please," Mark asked. I reluctantly followed him in.

He had built a little suite at the gym for his late nights there so he could just spend the night when he needed to.

"Can you clean up my room in here while I shut down the rest?" he asked.

"Sure," I said, though I felt hesitant.

Twenty minutes passed and I had finished cleaning. So I sat in the room waiting for him, though I was definitely ready to leave. He finally came back. As I grabbed my purse and coat to leave, he shut the door behind him and dimmed the lights. Every bad memory from almost a year ago rushed into my mind! I felt so foolish to be in the same position again.

"I need to go home Mark," I said to my boss.

"Lance and Julie already took off and I'm too drunk to drive, so I need to rest it off a bit first and then I'll take you home," he replied.

Sidenote: If you have ever been raped or molested, or someone even tried to do either to you, *tell someone*! Do not hesitate for any reason! Those who try this on others always have a great way of manipulating their victims or potential victims into feeling, for some reason, that they should not tell. No matter what, you did not deserve what that person tried or did to you. The only thing worse than what the person did to you or tried to do to you is him or her doing the same thing to someone else. I do not care if the person is a parent, coach, pastor, boyfriend — whoever — *you need to tell someone*! Tell someone who will listen and help you through a healing process. You are worth it!

I felt trapped. I had never been afraid of drunk driving before, and this night I definitely was not! I was more fearful of being imprisoned in his back room with him with no one else there to hear me or help me. He laid down on the small bed I was sitting on. I quickly stood up and he told me I had nothing to worry about, that he was just going to rest and I could turn the TV and watch whatever I wanted to. I sat back down and turned the TV on. I was happy to have it on as it brought more light into the room. While sitting there watching a movie, I considered calling someone to come and pick me up. But it was two in the morning and honestly, I was embarrassed about being there and did not want anyone to think anything, so I did not. Assuming he was asleep, I figured I would let him stay that way for an hour and then wake him up to take me home. I felt so manipulated—he was my boss!

Out of nowhere, he cuddled his head in my lap! *Oh no! What do I do now? He is passed out on my lap, and he is my boss. Do I push his head off me and get fired? Do I hope he tries nothing else and at work tomorrow pretend this never happened so things are not awkward?*

As my thoughts raced through my head, he threw his arm around me and shoved me back onto the bed! He moved his way up me and started kissing my neck and trying to take my clothes off. Once again, I felt fear come over me along with betrayal—that this was a grown man, my boss, doing this. Over and over I kept telling him no, but he would not stop. He kept telling me to relax and that he had envisioned this moment for so long. I was disgusted and wanted to run away from that room and the whole dreadful town. I kept pulling my clothes back on and trying to turn myself away from him. His drunken passion had kicked in and he was trying his hardest to force me to do what he wanted. Just as I most desperately hoped something or someone would save me from the situation I was in, the door cracked open and I saw a head peek in. It was Lance! He was still there. Mark had lied to me. I waved one of my hands at Lance, but it was dark in the room and my boss was still on top of me! I do not think he saw me because he quickly shut the door. I remember Lance having a disgusted look on his face that I felt was directed toward Mark. Perhaps I was not the first girl he had tried this on—nor the last he would try it on—and though Lance knew, he just did not want to get involved.

"Lance, come in!" I shouted quickly. Then I said to Mark, "Lance just opened the door."

Mark stopped abruptly and angrily fled to the door. Seeing my escape opportunity, I quickly got up, got my clothing situated, and ran right out the suite door, beating him to the exit door of the gym. I ran straight to Lance and said, " I'm ready to go home, right now!"

Mark interrupted, "I feel better now, I can take you."

I looked at Lance with pleading eyes, but I think he felt so awkward and disappointed, he did not know how to help me or to stand up to Mark. With grave reservations, I got into my bosses' car. I told him I needed to go straight home and that I was texting my dad that I was on way because he was worried about me. He knew it was over.

We did not say a word the entire drive to my house, which felt like an eternity. When we finally arrived, he said, "See you at work tomorrow?"

I looked at him puzzled because there was a weird tone in his voice, but I said, "Yes, of course."

Walking into my house I realized he was cluing me in to act as if what had happened that night never happened. I stayed quiet for a while, but I started hearing similar stories of this happening to other young girls and it was becoming obvious to everyone at the gym that he had issues! I wondered if it was as obvious to everyone that my life was out of control too.

Closing In

My parents could no longer overlook the changes in me. They were beginning to put the pieces together. I was losing even more weight, got in a fight at school with a girl and was suspended for three days, I never attended any family functions, and I had lost most of my drive for athletics and academics. The final straw was when the attendance office called my mom to ask why I had missed so many school days. They filled my mom in on the fact that they had a drawer full of notes signed by her, excusing me from many days of school. My mom told them she would be right in, of course, and that there was no way she had written all those notes. I was called into the attendance office. When I got there, I was surprised to see my mom sitting there with the office lady. My mom had a look on her face that could kill. They confronted me and I, of course, did not like that very much, so I looked my mom and the office lady in the face and said, "F-off!" Then I walked out, slamming the office door behind me.

I could feel my parents closing in on me and what was going on in my secretive life, but I was not ready to give in. Even though I was unhappy with where my choices were getting me, I did not want to be controlled. I quit the volleyball team in dramatic fashion, walking out on my coach and team. I could not keep my fake persona on anymore, so my last all-out binge was on its way. After all, everyone knew the "real" me anyway now, so why try to hide it anymore?

The summer before my senior year, I headed out one weekend to Eastern Washington, a vacation area, for Summer Jam. Three friends and I had plans to camp out with a bunch of other people, go to the concerts, and get plastered. However, three hours into our four-hour drive, my car started acting up. My AC quit working and was not blowing out any cool air. It was about one hundred degrees out and we were fried! Ultimately, we stripped down to our swimsuits. We were too excited about the weekend to care, so we drove along laughing and singing along to "The Thong Song," by Sisqo.

After several minutes, we noticed smoke billowing out from beneath the hood of my car! A semi-truck driver started waving us down to pull over, so we pulled over. I felt very uneasy about the driver because of all the horror stories my grandma had told me, but I had no choice. My car was about to blow up, I had no clue how to fix it, and we were out in the middle of nowhere! The driver pulled open the hood and we saw that my engine was actually on fire! We could have died from opening the hood! He put the fire out with the extinguisher from his truck, filled my car with all the fluids it needed, and then fixed a few other things. I was convinced then that the driver was a godsend. He said he thought we would be fine if we drove on the shoulder at a top speed of twenty mph. He told us that once I turned the car off, I would not be able to turn it back on or it might blow up. It took us about three hours to go sixty miles! He followed behind us the whole way to make sure we got there okay.

We were so happy when we arrived at the campground. We could finally party all weekend and have some fun! Many of our friends were already there, and they laughed at us as we pulled in. All evening more and more people pulled into the campground, but they knew people we knew, so we felt safe with them. We were a little leery of one group of crazy looking guys that rolled up in a big camper. Then I realized I had been out clubbing with Ariel, the girl-friend of the guy who owned the camper. Though she was not with them, the connection put me at ease. So we partied hard all weekend, drinking and mixing drugs.

When Monday morning came, we had to figure out how to get home since my car would not start. My friend Jenn and I had to get back for work, but our other friends planned to stay through the week, so we were having a hard time finding a ride back. I tried to start my car again, and it worked. But then the engine caught on fire again. My guy friends ran over quickly and put the fire out. I was just thankful it did not blow up! Just then, one of the guys from the camper we had partied with all weekend came forward and said he had driven out by himself and would take us home. Jenn jumped with joy, but I was honestly a bit nervous. I did not know why. After all, I had done much crazier things. I just did not feel good about the guy. We went with him anyway.

I told Jenn how I felt and she assured me everything would be fine. My deal in going was, I got the door side and she had to sit in the middle by him. I was pretty much silent or sleeping the whole trip back. When I awoke, we were close to Seattle, but I noticed he had turned a different direction than where I told him we lived. I woke Jenn up and told her what was going on, so she told him, "We need to go the other way. We live back the other direction," she said, pointing behind us.

"I need to stop by my place first," he said.

I quickly spoke up. "We don't have time for that. We have to get to our jobs. Please take us straight home."

"It will be quick and then I will take you home," he insisted.

I had the worst feeling inside me. Fear gripped me. I wondered how I always managed to get myself into such dreadful situations. I thought how much better it would have been for us to have simply chosen not to go to work that day and stay with our friends. At least we would not have been at risk of winding up dead like we were now!

We pulled into his apartment complex and he got out and invited us in. I declined with a no thank you and said my boss was expecting me soon. He looked at Jenn and asked her if she would go in with him. I poked her to let her know, *no way!* Smiling sweetly, she kindly replied that she would wait patiently outside. He slammed the door and went in for five minutes. I told Jenn how nervous I was and that I felt really bad about this. We wondered if we should jump out of his car, but she assured me again that if he took us home, we could make it to work on time. I listened to her.

He returned and got into the car without saying a word. I pretended to be on the phone with my boss, telling him I was on my way in to work after getting a ride from a nice guy. (I said that hoping to manipulate him.) He dropped me off first, and I told Jenn to call me as soon as she got home. She called soon afterward and I took a deep breath. I wondered where all the terrible feelings that gripped me on that trip had come from, but could not pinpoint it. After a few days, I forgot all about that guy and the trip home.

About a month later, I got a frightening call from a friend telling me to turn on the news. A picture of Ariel, the beautiful girlfriend of the guy who owned the camper, was on the TV screen. Someone had kidnapped Ariel, tortured her for days, and then brutally murdered her in the mountains with a gunshot to her head. Next, I saw a picture of her boyfriend and two of his buddies . . . including the guy who had driven Jenn and I home! The news anchor reported that all three had raped her and tortured her for days in her boyfriend's garage before taking her to the mountains and killing her. I could not believe it. I had goose bumps all over my body! I could not believe Ariel had died, and in such a horrible way. I freaked out, realizing how close Jenn and I had come to that happening to us. We had been in a car with him for hours!

The news broadcaster went on to say that the men had been planning what they did to Ariel for close to a year. They also had a long list of other people they planned to murder after her. Again, I had that feeling something was protecting me and watching out for me. Still, I kept on living the same lifestyle. It was almost as if I was racing against time to get away with as much as I could before it ran out.

I felt my life was on the verge of some kind of an end. My parents had to find out about my car because I had to leave it where it broke down. I explained to them part of what had happened, but left out most of the story. However, they were not stupid. They were learning that my dad had no control over me, I had no rules or discipline in my life, and the school had had enough of my deception and I was costing them money. My parents had almost had enough. I am not sure why that was not the last straw for them. Perhaps I had to finish my wild streak or hit "rock bottom" as people call it, but it was not over . . . not yet!

CHAPTER 5
"ROCK BOTTOM"

As if all that had happened was not enough for me, my poor parents, family, and everyone close to me, I hit high gear. But then something more powerful than me brought on a wild series of events that changed my life—literally changed my entire life! There was no way for me to understand the events at the time. I just knew I was not quite crazy, and whatever was happening to me was real.

My boyfriend Jack continued to cheat on me. We were continually on or off and I often resorted to trying to hurt him back by kissing other guys, but I had created a soul tie with a disease—something I did not want anymore but could not get rid of. In fact, I had not felt love in a long time in our relationship. It was more about pride and conquering what was mine (or what I thought was mine).

The end of summer was fast approaching, and I was in my junior year of high school. Weekends were usually my time to let loose with my friends and do whatever I wanted. Whatever I did, the goal was to not think about Jack and what he was doing, but about being crazy with my friends and being "free"!

One weekend, my close friends and I jumped into a truck and went out to party. Just as we pulled up to the first party my friend, Larry, pulled out a huge bag of ecstasy! I had never seen that much ecstasy before. He said he bought it all to sell it and could get fifty dollars a pill because it was so strong! Naturally, we decided to try some first. We were so excited to try the new stronger pills. Larry and my best guy friend, Freddy, were in the front seat of the truck, crushing the pills and giving lines to my girlfriend Natalie and I, in the back. We went into the party for a while and the ecstasy began to hit us hard. We were having a great time until we hear that the neighbors had called the cops on us for being too loud. We all sprinted out to our vehicles and hightailed it out of there.

When we pulled up to the next party I saw Larry looking first all over the car and then in his coat and pockets for something.

"Larry, what are you looking for?" I asked.

"I don't know where the 'f-in' bag went!" he yelled. "Help me look for it! That's a lot of 'f-in' money!"

We thought he was messing with us because we did not understand how anyone could accidentally lose that big of a bag of ecstasy! But he was high, so anything was possible. We jumped back into the truck and sped back toward the first house, retracing our route. We looked and looked but could not find it. Finally, in the driveway of the house we saw the bag in the driveway. Larry quickly walked over to the bag and picked it up. The ecstasy inside had been crushed to powder! He had run it over with his huge truck when we left. He could not sell a crushed product. All that money, wasted. None of us had that kind of money except for him. His dad was rich, so Larry had and got anything he ever wanted or needed. Larry was so high that he cussed only for a minute before he started laughing and said, "Let's get higher than we ever have tonight!"

We were down, of course. We went back to the party at the other house and sat in the driveway, snorting line after line. He sneaked me extra lines — not sure why — but I did not hesitate to take them. He always bought my drugs and alcohol and slipped me extra things, and I took it happily.

Earlier that night, at the first party, we had been drinking, doing drugs, and snorting some lines, before the cops came. We were already pretty much out of it, but we started taking lines fearlessly, never stopping to think, *Is that enough?* We were like kids in a candy store! We had what seemed an unlimited amount of one of the strongest drugs available.

We went into the party for a bit, but tons of people were piling in and the girl who owned the house was beyond stressed. We decided to leave. It was not our group anyway. We headed to a third place, an apartment owned by people I did not know.

On the way there, I felt all the drugs kick in to the extreme. I felt I had no control over my body. I could think, but my body felt disconnected from me. I felt unable to move my legs, arms, or even turn my head. I could not control the expressions on my face, and I definitely could not talk. I somehow made it up the stairs to the apartment, but could not remember how. I went in and sat down on their couch right away. Voices sounded fuzzy and my eyes saw everything as if I was looking through one of those rounded windows in an aquarium. I could see only the very middle of what I looked at; everything around it looked blurry. I could not tell the actual size of anything. Things far away seemed close and things close seemed far away. A fuzzy glare was on everything I could still see.

The couple who lived in the apartment had a two-year-old little girl. I love children—always have. I remember that little girl captured my heart in the middle of my high. After Larry said he was going to the kitchen to smoke a bowl with his friends, they yelled at the little girl, telling her, "You know where to go when we pull this out (their bong)!" The little girl obediently ran into the living room and crouched by my legs. They yelled at her to start picking up the living room. She began picking up the pillows off the floor and putting them on the couch. In spite of how strong my trip was, I was shocked that a little two-year-old was around us and all this stuff! My heart was broken for how her parents treated her. This was my second major feeling of conviction; the first being the night Danielle was raped by those men. This little girl was too innocent to be around this! I reached my arms out for her to hold her but missed. At that point I was seeing multiples of her. I tried three times, but missed each time. I was finally able to get out a few words and asked her to come to me. She walked over to me and climbed up in my lap, and I wrapped my arms around her.

Freddy came over to me and sat down beside me. "Heather, are you okay?" he asked me. That was the last thing I remember. I passed out.

Later on, they told me Freddy carried me to the truck and put me in the front seat. Larry drove us home. We stopped at Freddy's house first because my dad's house was farther away, outside of town. Freddy told Larry to get me home right away because he was really worried about me. I had been unconscious for a while and had not moved or made a sound. Larry assured Freddy he would get me home. However, on the way to my house, I apparently started to foam at the mouth. This freaked Larry out. He thought I was dead and that he would be blamed for giving me all the drugs, so he turned the truck around and started driving me back toward Seattle. His dad owned many apartment buildings all over the area and some were abandoned, awaiting remodel. He brought me to one of the abandoned buildings, carried me up to one of the apartments, and left me on the floor of a room, like trash.

I do not remember anything that happened that night from the moment I passed out until three days later. I believe with all my heart that I really was dead.

"I believe with all my heart that I really was dead."

The school district called my mom and let her know I had not been to school for a couple days. My mom called my dad. He did not know where I was. My mom threatened him, saying that he had better find me or she was going to call the police and do whatever it took to get me back. There was no way my dad wanted to go through any more legal battles with my mom, or deal with the police, so he called Freddy right away.

"Where's Heather? She hasn't been home in days!"

"Larry was supposed to have brought her home Saturday night," Freddy told him. "That was the last time I saw her."

"Find her and bring her home ASAP, Freddy! You are supposed to be watching after her!" my dad yelled.

Freddy called Larry and pressed him and pressed him until Larry gave in and said he would take him to where I was. They drove back down toward Seattle, about forty-five minutes away from where we lived. They pulled into the apartment complex and ran up the stairway to the room where Larry had left me to die. I was still lying there on the floor. Freddy must have thought I was dead because they began to argue. As they argued, I gained consciousness for the first time. I could barely hear Freddy's voice, but heard him cussing out Larry and pushing him around. Then through the crack of the door, Freddy saw me move just a little. He rushed in and picked me up off the floor.

They brought me home. I did not remember any of the drive, until we pulled into my driveway. Once there, Freddy carried me to my room and put me in my bed. I remember my dad just glaring at me as we walked by him, everyone was sick me now including my dad.

I was never the best daughter to my dad. I spoke to him awful and I had no respect for him. I had witnessed all his drama with his girlfriends — the cheating; the screaming girlfriends pounding on our door, trying to get into our house, and more. I had seen him get physically abusive with girls. I had been drunk with my dad plenty of times. He had provided alcohol and drugs for my friends and I. Though I liked the fact that I could get away with anything, I had no respect for him because of it. Still, I could not blame him for my life. I actually used his faults as excuses to do whatever I wanted. Ultimately, I had made my own decisions. I was where I was because of my own rebellion and bad choices.

**"I was where I was because of my own rebellion
and bad choices."**

Alive

I slept for a full day and night. I got up and got ready for school the following day, but still felt completely out of it. I was still unsure what had happened to me over the last few days. It felt so strange, walking into school that day. It felt like I was walking into a brand new place where I knew no one. I wondered if anyone knew what was going on in me. I feared they might know me better than I knew myself.

To my surprise, in health class that morning, it was "Drug Day"! Coincidence? I am not sure, but it did not feel unintentional. They showed a video. To my shock, it was a about a sixteen-year-old boy who had overdosed on ecstasy! At one point, the image of a huge ecstasy pill crossed the screen. When I saw the symbol on it I could not believe it — it was a picture of the same ecstasy I had done. Then they showed the dead boy being wheeled out on a stretcher as his mom screamed and cried over the loss of her son. It was too much, too fast. I began to weep out loud in the back of the classroom. A couple of people turned around to me to ask if I was okay, but I just kept my head down, crying. I just knew I should not have been sitting there right then . . . I should have been dead. I was so grateful to be alive.

After school that day, I had a doctor appointment to get a drug test. I was full of anxiety as I waited for the results in a cold room for a long time. Finally, the doctor and a nurse came in with the test results. They both looked me straight in the eye as the doctor said, "You are a walking dead person! You have more than enough drugs in your system to kill three grown men!"

I was in shock. They had confirmed what I feared. I started to cry again. I did not understand how I was still alive! Though I was a little nervous about failing the drug test, knowing it could be turned in to the police department, I was overwhelmingly thankful to be sitting there in that moment, alive, whether I got in trouble or not.

That day, I quit doing all hard drugs. No seven-step programs required. I just quit cold turkey. It was a miracle! Though partly inspired by fear of failing future drug tests and trouble with the police, ultimately, I knew I had to stop if I wanted to stay alive and could not shake the feeling that something was giving me another chance.

However, I was still not ready to give up everything. I still drank and smoked weed because, in high school, we were dumb enough to believe (or at least tell ourselves) weed was not a drug! I learned this revelation a little late: Anything that makes you see funny things, feel funny things, and alters your normal self *is a drug*! Slowly but surely, the layers of my wild lifestyle began to peel away like an onion.

Sidenote: Weed is a drug. *Period.* Weed should not be legalized. *Period.* Our problem in America—and as humans—is that we are obsessed with making excuses for ourselves to live the way we want and as *comfortably* as possible with no consequences. As long as we continue to push back the lines between right and wrong, the more consequences we will receive, not just individually, but as a nation. We make excuses for ourselves to compromise. It is one thing to make a bad decision and do the wrong thing, but it is a whole other thing to call the wrong thing *right*! We need our morality back. We need to stop confusing ourselves with the many excuses people use to try and make it okay to do the wrong thing "if this" or "if that" happens. No! *Morality is all about choosing to do the right thing even if it is the hard thing to do!* Morality aside, would you want to drive down any road with cars full of high people? The bad decisions of other people do affect all of us. *"If you give an inch, they take a mile."*

Moving Day

Shortly after my drug overdose, my mom gave my dad a heads up that she was headed to his house, and she was bringing cops with her. My dad yelled at me that my mom was on her way over with the cops. I ran for the bathroom, locked myself inside, and tried my best to barricade the door. I was willing to fight to the very end to stay in control over my messed up life. When the cops arrived, they pounded on the door, shouting: "Open this door right now! You have about five seconds to open this door! If you don't, we will tear down this door and take you to jail!" My mom yelled behind them, showing her support by shouting, "I won't be rescuing you from jail, and neither will your dad, so open the door . . . now!"

They had all had enough of me. I contemplated what to do for a long time. They were patient cops. They probably felt bad for my poor mom. Finally, after they gave me the last ultimatum, I moved everything out of the way of the door and got the courage to open the door. Opening the door with cops on the other side did not scare me; giving up control terrified me. I had worked so hard to make my life what I wanted it to be — no matter how foolish and destructive it was. I feared what was ahead of me, especially giving up my *"freedom."* I was fearful of the *truth* and admitting how I was wrong and what I needed to *change*. Looking back now, it seems so weird to be fearful of my *salvation*.

The police told me to get in the back of their car so they would escort me to my mom's house, but I refused and jumped into the back of my mom's car. I was still fighting for any last bit of control I could. They followed us home until we pulled into the driveway. Before leaving, one officer shouted out his window to my mom, telling her to call him if I tried anything. I was trapped. I went up to my room and barricaded myself in. I moved my dresser and every other piece of furniture in my room in front of that door. "You can't stay in there forever!" my mom yelled in at me.

"Looking back now, it seems so weird to be fearful of my salvation."

With my last bit of fight, I chose to try to prove her wrong. That night and the whole next day went by. I refused to come out or let anyone in. I was starving, but the last bit of inner rebellion in me was not going to let me lose the battle and open the door. My parents turned off my electricity, cable, and heat to force me to open. I did not care.

Late the next night, while lying on my floor, I heard my grandparents' voices as they came through the front door. Now I was worried. I loved and respected my grandparents (my mom's parents) so much I could not yell at them or disrespect them. There is just something about the elderly — especially your own grandparents — you do not want to disappoint them. They were the only people I had never disrespected and I was embarrassed for them to see me like that. They were so naive. They knew nothing I had done except the little my mom had told them. My papa asked me nicely to open the door, but I stayed on the floor, crying. Then I heard my grandma shove my papa out of the way and start banging her fist loudly on my door. "Open this door right now, Heather Lynn!" she screamed. "I'm not asking, I'm telling you to open it now! Do you hear me? Open this door right now!" My grandma could be a scary person if she wanted to be. (My mom and I got our warrior spirits from her!) With another slam on the door from her, I popped up, moved everything out of the way and opened the door.

My grandparents took me out to dinner that night and talked with me. I know my mom was not happy that they came in as the heroes, but it softened my heart some. It was the beginning for me to begin working on letting my guard down. Now that everyone had experienced me at my worst, there was no more dodging to do. I soon got honest with myself and realized I was happy my mom had forced my rescue (not that I would have actually told her that at the time!). Had my mom not taken action when she did, I am not sure I would have lived much longer.

I-5

Still, I did have one more close call. One night, I snuck out of my mom's house and met up with my old party friends (except Freddy), including Larry, the guy who left me for dead in the abandoned apartment. We made our way to a party, though I made it clear I would not be doing any drugs. I offered to be the DD (Designated Driver). Some of them were irritated with me about my "sudden change," so they treated me like a traitor. They lied to me about things they were doing, including the drugs they were using. This seriously hurt me since we had been so close and gone through so much together. I did not want to have to break off my friendships despite the fact that they no longer seemed to trust me simply because I had decided to make a positive change in my life. Sometimes my loyalty to people has nearly been my undoing.

Side Note: If you need healing from any kind of addiction in your life (mentally, emotionally, etc.), right now, know *you* need to love *you* first before you can love others. Your loyalty to other people cannot be more important than getting yourself healthy. I am not talking about selfishness and always putting yourself before others. What I am saying, just as I would if I were face to face with you: Kick them to the curb! Some people think I am being harsh when I advise this, insisting that their friends need their help. I respond by asking, "How can a broken person fix a broken person?" Honestly, very few people want their friend who has done drugs/alcohol/whatever with them forever to tell them they ought to quit and become a better person! *You* need to take care of *you* and *anyone* who is not one hundred percent supportive (*respectful*) of your life change needs to stay out of your life — at least for a long, extended period of time.

This brings me to my next point: Do not get better for three months and then go call everybody back up again to hang with them as if you are all better! You may feel better, but the unhealthy pattern of living you created over years will not change that quickly. Your heart, mind, and spirit have to follow along fully with your new change for quite some time. It is not just about behavior change, it is about *life* change.

**"It is not just about behavior change,
it is about *life* change."**

As to your friends who need help: find someone else to help them—anyone other than you! You need to take care of *you* so you can be a *better you*. One day you will help others, but it will be when everything in you is the *new you*.

We arrived at the party and went in for a while. Larry went back into a room somewhere with a guy I did not know. I noticed everyone was acting a little funny toward me and not really talking to me. The next thing I knew, a bunch of people came running from a back bedroom screaming, "The cops are on their way and almost here!" We all took off running to our cars. Everyone in my car said they had not done any drugs, so I jumped in the back seat. It all happened so quickly.

We started driving toward my home, but we had at least an hour's drive ahead of us. I was tired and ready to go to bed, so I got too comfortable in the back seat and fell asleep. Little did I know, the guy in the back with me and Ashley in the front seat had fallen asleep as well. Shortly after we had all fallen asleep, Larry, our driver, also passed out! I just remember being jerked awake and looking out the windshield and realizing Larry had driven off the freeway going north, down an embankment, over a ditch, and into oncoming traffic! We were driving north on I-5 South! Left and right, cars were honking and splitting off the road at 65 mph as we drove down the middle of the freeway! I yelled, "Larry!" and grabbed the wheel and turned it sharply, causing us to crash into a ditch. All of us but Ashley were awake now and wondering what had happened. I was breathing so hard I could not say anything. As I tried to catch my breath, Larry jumped out of the car to check it. While he was outside, I questioned the guy beside me about what they had all taken at the party. He said they had been ripped off by a dealer—he had sold them all sleeping pills! I was so pissed that they had all lied to me! I looked at Ashley and was surprised to see she was still sleeping in spite of all we had just gone through. Larry opened the car door and informed us that we had a flat tire. I just wanted to be home, but here I was again, stuck in a regretful situation due to my bad choices.

I waited in the car as Ashley snored in the front seat. The guys ran across five lanes of traffic to get an air pump for the tire. While they were gone, which felt like an eternity, I had an eventful time guarding our car, my friend, and my freedom.

Thankful for a Sweatshirt

First, I saw the headlights of a car coming up behind our car, filling it with light. The car pulled over and parked right behind us. I could see there was one man in the car. My mind raced, *What in the world is this guy doing at 1 a.m., pulling over behind us?* I watched through the back window as he got out of his car, and he looked cray-cray—like seriously "craz-ay"! My heart sped back up again as he walked up to our car. He banged on the windows, screamed profanities, and asked what we were doing. I was scared out of my mind! Being as brave as I was, I hid my face under a sweatshirt on the floor and said my first prayer in a really long time. After pounding on the windows for about five minutes, which felt like forever, he finally left. I took a deep breath, but stayed under the sweatshirt, just in case he was still standing outside my window. Only after I heard him start his car and pull back onto the freeway did I come out from hiding. Phew! I was so relieved . . . for the moment.

Moments later, I heard sirens and saw lights flashing in the rear-view mirror. I could not believe it. My heart began to race even faster than before. It was a miracle I did not have a heart attack. I just knew this was it—I was going to be arrested for my friends' stupidity, and neither one of them would have come to my rescue if they saw a cop arresting Ashley or I.

The cop tapped on the driver's window with his flashlight and told me to roll down the window, so I did. He turned his flashlight on and pointed it directly into my eyes. I put my whole body in front of the window to hide my friend and covered up the empty cans of beer on the floor with the sweatshirt I had used earlier to hide my face. I rolled down the window just a bit.

"Is everything okay?" the officer asked.

"Ah, yes, everything is fine, sir. We just have a flat tire and my friends ran over to the gas station to get a pump to fix it."

He directed his flashlight over to our flat tire to check out what I said.

"Are you sure? And what about your friend?" he pried.

"She is just tired because it's so late. Really, we are fine!" I assured him.

He stared at the car and then stared at me, perhaps trying to decide whether to believe me or not. I interrupted his thought process and said with a big smile on my face, "Thank you so much for stopping though, and for your concern!" With that, he walked away, got back into his car, and drove away. Whew . . . another close call!

I leaned back in my seat, closed my eyes and took another few deep breaths. I realized how mad I was at the guys at that point, I could have killed them for putting me in that position and taking so long! They were probably eating candy and nachos while I had risked being kidnapped and arrested! I looked out the window for them and saw them running back across the freeway, laughing hysterically about something. (The last thing I felt like doing was laughing!)

The guys finally made it back and started working on the tire. I tried to wait patiently, but then I heard them cussing and laughing again. I opened my door to see what was going on and asked, "What the hell are you two idiots doing? Is the tire fixed yet?"

Still laughing, they said, "We just broke the f-ing air can! Now what?"

I felt like crying, but did not. We were screwed. Larry then came up with the brilliant idea of driving home on the flat tire, even though we were fifty miles from home. This lasted about two minutes. (It did not help that he took off at 60 mph!) The rubber flew off and we were driving on the metal rim with sparks flying out the back end of the car. Talk about attracting a cop! The only thing worse than sitting on the side of the freeway with a flat tire is driving down the freeway with sparks flying from your rim.

"Stop!" I yelled. "Pull over now!"

We all started fighting. We did not know what to do. It was now like 3 a.m. and no one was coming to our rescue . . . well, except for Larry's mom, our very last resort, but only option. She lived thirty miles away. She was an interesting character. The good news was, we knew we would not be in trouble for what we had been up to – she was not that *type* of mom. We just hoped she would show up.

We sat and waited a half hour for her to arrive, and once she did, we all piled into her little car. We made it back to her apartment at about 4 a.m. All I wanted was my bed, and I knew I was in for it when my parents woke up in the morning and saw I was not there! It was the first time I desired to be home in my own bed. I noticed that night that my desires were changing. I did not crave the rebellious, crazy, party life anymore – I was actually kind of sick of it. I could not wait to get home in the morning, even if that meant I would be grounded.

Sadly, it took many events to break my will and the habits I had formed over the previous four years. But I was thankful for these *events.* They were *supernatural* and *changed* me.

Voices

I was on my way up to visit my boyfriend, Jack, at his college. I took a couple of friends with me that I had not hung out with for a while since I was trying to stay away from drugs (though as I wrote earlier, we did not think of weed as a drug).

We got to Jack's place and all sat down to smoke a bowl together. I was one of the last people in our circle of five. After everyone else had taken a hit, my friend passed me the pipe and, I kid you not, the moment I grabbed it, the whole room *froze!* Everyone was frozen in mid-conversation. I could not believe it! What was going on with me? Then I heard a *voice* asking me questions: "Is this what you *dreamed* about doing when you were a child? Are you really *happy* living like this? Do you want your *future* to look like this?"

These were really good questions I had not asked myself before. But where were these questions coming from?

I could not believe what was happening. I did not understand what was happening. Behind the questions, I heard a quiet voice say over and over, "No, no, no, no, no, no . . ." Then just as suddenly as the room had frozen, it unfroze and everyone resumed what they had been doing. I just interrupted and blurted out, "No!"

They all stopped and stared at me. "What do you mean, no?" they asked.

"I mean, no! I'm done! I quit! I'm not doing this anymore!"

They laughed at me they said, "Ah, you're just already high Heather. Sit down and chill and smoke with us."

"I told you I'm done! I'll prove it to you!" I said defensively. My competiveness was finally kicking in for some good!

"Heather, we all know you'll be right back here with us next weekend smoking again, so you might as well do it now," one of them said.

I was pissed, so I stood up and walked out. I knew I was done—forever. I felt it. I did not want it anymore. And from that moment on, I never touched it again! I had smoked weed just about every day for four years straight, and I stopped at that moment.

I know this story brings us back to the beginning of this whole story, but it was really an ending and new beginning for me. I stood up for the first time, wanting to do the right thing. A "new will" was manifesting through me.

Side Note: The human will is stronger than we think. We ultimately do what we want to do, whether we admit this or not. It truly is our decision to live life the way we want to. It is something totally different to blame the life we live on someone or something else. We all have a will and we all willingly live the way we choose. We all may grow up in different types of households, have different devastating circumstances that play into the path we have chosen, but anyone at any time can choose a different path. You do not have to be what others say they think you are. You do not have to live the life they think you should. You can make the decision to *change* and get help. However, to do that, you cannot make excuses for yourself or accept them from others. Our flesh will always try to convince us to stay where we are at, but our soul and heart cry out for something better. Listen to your heart. Do not make excuses for yourself, no matter what your past was like. Your future can be what you make it.

The world has made the word *change* a negative word. No one wants to hear anymore that they need to change. Why? Because it is easier to settle and just keep on doing what we have been doing and being who we have been. It is easier to not have to work on ourselves. It is true that it is so much easier to stay right where we are and be who we are right now. But what if something inside you is crying out for more, crying out for *change*?

"You do not have to be what others say they think you are."

If you are really about being different, then do not do what the world tells you to do! When everyone does that . . . they all end up the same! The world says, "Don't be *judgmental!*" If you love them, you will not make them change, you will love them the way they are." I say, "I love you the way you are, but if *you* love *you*, make the positive changes in your life to be the best you and who you were *created* to be!" Just because I disagree with someone's lifestyle or decision does not mean I am judgmental! Judgment is casting a sentence! I am prejudging if I say in my mind: *That person (I do not know) is wearing baggy pants and wearing a bandana on their head. They must be a gang member. I should stay away from them.* If I say to my friend (whom I know), "Do not go out with that guy tonight, you already have a boyfriend," I am not judging her! I am being a *real* friend by telling her the *truth* and giving her my counsel. We have twisted this whole "judging" thing so that nobody can tell us what we do not want to hear. It is a narcissistic way of life to never allow critique or people who love you or care for you to bring warning your way! We all have issues. We are all in process. So *change* does not have to be a scary or negative word. I gladly and fearlessly invite change into my life!

When I stood and walked out of that room, I felt a bit bizarre because I did not understand what had just happened to me. It was supernatural, something that no one would ever be able to believe — at least not the people around me at the time.

Soon after, a friend of mine, Amanda, asked me to go to the mall with her that weekend to shoplift. We often did this. It was normal for us to go out during the day and steal a few new outfits for the week, especially for clubbing. We would bring huge, empty, boxy shopping bags and put one of our own shirts in to pretend we had bought things. We would go into stores, grab clothes, and take them into the changing rooms to pretend to try them on. Instead, we ripped the sensors off the clothes, shoved them into our bags, and just walked out with new wardrobes. When my mom questioned me about all my new clothing, I would tell her my dad had taken me shopping, which she believed. He spoiled us by buying us things to win our favor. (She was too naive to notice the holes in the garments from us ripping out the sensors.)

Amanda and I confirmed our plan to go to the mall with one other friend, Tasha. The weekend came. When I woke up that Saturday morning, I felt a pressing feeling not to go. It was weird, like when people say their conscience talks to them. I ignored the feeling and jumped into the shower to get ready to go. However, the whole time I was getting ready, the daunting feeling just got stronger and stronger. Then I began hearing a *voice* say, "Don't go!" over and over, just as the voice had spoken to me at my boyfriend's place. The only difference was that this time, I really wanted to go with my friends and the voice was getting really annoying, like a ringing in my ear. It would not stop, so I finally slammed my hands down on the bathroom counter and yelled at myself in the mirror, saying, "Shut up! I'm going!" Now I really felt psycho—I was not only talking to myself, but yelling at myself! (Or was it really myself?). Whatever was happening, it was getting on my last nerve because I was going with my friends to the mall no matter what. My friends finally got to my house to pick me up and I left, passing my mom on the way out. She was not worried since I was only going to the mall and not a crack house or bar.

We got to the mall and started doing our thing. The only problem was, at the first store we went into, I felt oddly distracted and could not steal anything! We left the store and went to the next one . . . and the same odd thing happened! Amanda and Tasha start questioning me about why I was not stealing anything. I had no answer for them so I lied and told them I was not feeling well.

We decided to go into a big department store we all liked and I made my mind up that I would steal something there for sure. We all went our separate ways and I found myself standing before a sweater I can still picture in my mind today. I loved it, wanted it, and was ready to steal it! I reached out for it on the rack and all of a sudden, my arm felt weighed down and smacked my thigh! I stood in shock. *Did I just have a muscle spasm?* I tried again and my arm was driven down, hitting my thigh again. I was already in shock from the first time, so I could not go any further into shock, but if it were possible I would have! I stood there trying over and over again to take the sweater off the rack, but I was physically unable to do it! I'm not sure how long I sat there and tested that crazy power, but it was enough time for my friends to get clothes off of the racks, go into the changing rooms, rip sensors off, shove the clothes into their bags, and come find me. I had lost all sense of time, but my guess is that I sat in front of that one sweater for thirty minutes trying to take it off the rack over and over!

Can you imagine if anyone had been watching me during that time? Ha! Hysterical. I cannot imagine what that must have looked like, or what they must have thought. I had no answers and was in shock myself.

I was snapped out of my stunned comatose by Amanda and Tasha tapping me on the shoulders saying, "Let's go!" The three of us started toward the entrance of the store to make our exit, Tasha on my left, Amanda on my right. Before we stepped out of the store, I was frightened by the sounds and sight of my friends being taken down to the floor, yelled at, and handcuffed. As I looked down at them in shock, the police officers looked at me and told me to keep walking. Where was I to go? They were my friends and my only way home! I sat in the middle of the mall, humbled as I watched my friends being walked out of the store and then loaded into police cars.

I, the "innocent one," had to call my friends' parents. I did not understand why it did not happen to me. Over and over I had tried to steal, not knowing we were being watched the *entire time*! I was worse than both of them, and here I was, not being handcuffed. What was going on?

In my brokenness, I suddenly recalled my childhood, being raised in church, and believing in God and his Son Jesus Christ, who died on the cross for our sins (my sins). I could think of no reason for this supernatural series of events other than God was working in some way. I knew for sure I was never ever going to steal again. In that moment complete fear came over me. Honestly, in my whole life, I had never been fearful until I overdosed and then experienced this crazy sequence of events. I remembered the *voice* asking if I was ready to be done. Was I ready to be done? Like *done* done? Like *really actually done done done*?

One More Thing

The final and only thing that had not been ripped out of my life was my unhealthy relationship with my boyfriend. I had wanted to break up with him for a while, but never had the strength in me to follow through. I did not want to hurt his feelings, though he had never cared about my feelings. He had also successfully manipulated me, saying he would kill himself (and many other ridiculous things), if I ever left him. He was trying to scare me into staying with him! What kind of relationship is that?

One night, convinced I was finished with him, I realized I needed help to follow through on breaking up with Jack. At the time, since I had moved back in with my mom and stepdad, they made me go back to church with them on Sundays. I had been hearing a lot about prayer, so I decided I would try to pray about the breakup while lying in bed. It was a funny prayer that I did not take seriously. I prayed, "God, if you're really real and really can do whatever you want, then make me physically ill to the point I can't stand to be around Jack or even hear his voice." Then I fell asleep.

The next day, I completely forgot about the prayer and went to school and followed my new normal routine. A few days later, Jack called me and invited me over to his house to watch a movie. As we talked I suddenly began to feel very sick.

You may be thinking, *No way! Seriously?* Yes, I am as serious as a heart attack! I came down with the flu (or at least flu-like symptoms)! On my way over to his house, I felt nauseous the whole time, but still did not remember my prayer from a couple nights ago. I got to his house and right when he opened the door, I explained to him that I felt very sick. We sat down on the couch and he tried to put his arm around me, and right as he did I had to get up and run to the bathroom! I immediately started dry heaving. After a few more runs to the toilet, and him feeling offended by me telling him not to touch me because I felt too sick, it hit me! This was God genuinely answering my prayers!

I could not believe it. God had actually acknowledged me and answered me! *But wait . . . I believe in God? Well of course I do, I guess.* I had been taught about him growing up, but had never thought about him or him actually being a part of my life. I felt less sick for a moment as I realized how real God was! There was a real God, not a boring history class kind of God. He was not a peaceful creature who once lived and healed people . . . he is real today, right now! And he is still powerful!

"God had actually acknowledged me and answered me!"

I left Jack's house, telling him I felt too sick and would be back when I felt better. I knew I would never feel better while with him or looking at him. Ha! It was like the moment in the story of Scrooge when he opened his eyes realizing he had been given a second chance to live a better life. I had my second chance — well, third, fourth, and fifth chance — but I was thankful for them now! I now understood all the crazy things that had been happening to me (in a small way at least). I was not crazy — they were not all coincidences. I was convinced God was *real* and watching out for me. (This was definitely not a job I would have wanted — and a busy one at that!)

However, there was something more to this than God just answering my prayer; it was like . . . God spoke back to me! God answered me. *Wait, God answered me?* I did not even know he could really do that! I think I felt loved for the first time in a very long time. It felt so good! But still I wondered, *Why me?*

CHAPTER 6
ONE-EIGHTY

I attended church with my mom and stepdad on a consistent basis. I began to build a good relationship with both of them, in fact, it quickly went from good to great! The anger and rebellion were leaving me. I wanted no part of it anymore. My heart felt soft and healed of so many wounds. All of a sudden, I loved my stepdad. I had never noticed all he had sacrificed to take care of all of us, and I became very appreciative. I felt so awful for the way I had treated my mom and dad. I had taken advantage of them in every way and lied to them for years! I had been blind, but my eyes had been opened and I could see clearly. Finally, I could feel love. All of a sudden, things were very different!

One day after church, as I ran into the house all excited about the service that day, I remember my mom saying to me, "Where is my daughter and what have you done with her?" Everyone around me was in shock over my dramatic change. It was a miracle how dramatically my life had changed from one month to the next!

My friends did not recognize me either! They did not know how to treat me or talk to me. They invited me to parties every once in a while, thinking I missed that life, but I really did not. I did miss some of my relationships, but I wanted nothing that came with them. I knew they were still stuck in that lifestyle, and I wanted to pull them out, but I realized they could not see it—they were blind to it (just as I had been for so long). They were not ready to be saved from it yet, and I knew I was not strong enough to carry them while still trying to change myself. It was definitely hard for me. I wanted them to experience what I had experienced, but I just knew in my heart I needed a full "makeover" before I started trying to help transform anyone else.

I quickly found out that I could not change others if they did not want to change (consider my life!). I fought it the whole way until my mom forced me (with the help of heavenly intervention), for my own good. (Oh, how thankful I was for that!) Not everyone is willing to submit, even when the forceful approach is used on them. Sometimes peoples' lives are so dark that they cannot see the light of even the smallest amount of hope. I was grateful there was still a small flame burning in me . . . it saved me.

"I quickly found out that I could not change others if they did not want to change. . ."

Still, my past was trying hard to hold me back. Though I had made great progress very quickly, the fight had just begun! So many temptations surrounded me. However, I was on cloud nine, which made me vulnerable to deception.

It was my senior year, and all the senior parties were being planned: graduation, prom, and so on. I was nervous, but more than ever before I felt a strong stance inside of me: I did not want any of the alcohol, drugs, or sex anymore. I soon realized that I had never wanted any of it. I wanted the respect and attention it brought me, so I ended up a *slave* to those things to get what I wanted from others. The *freedom* part of it all was deceiving because "my freedom" was destroying my life. That is what *rebellion*, is all about; fighting for a freedom that is not real, but destructive.

"The *freedom* part of it all was deceiving because "my freedom" was destroying my life."

Sidenote: Rebellion refuses to take counsel, receive help, or submit to what is best. It tells you that you have to do it all on your own, to run away from every healthy relationship, those that truly love you and makes you crave what you know is not good for you. The only way to kill it is through *humility*.

What is humility? Humility is about lowering yourself, getting rid of pride and that puffed up defensive thing that rises up in us. Humility is about receiving help and guidance, and following through with them. Humility is about *submitting* to the *process* (no one is fixed overnight). It means listening to the hard stuff we do not want to hear, but we do it to better ourselves.

Everyone has weaknesses, but those who *overcome* their weaknesses are willing to *see* them and work on them. Humility is also about admitting when we are wrong and apologize to those we have hurt. It takes responsibility for the wrong things we have done. Humility is not a lot of fun, but I promise you, it will change your life.

There is something about humbling yourself, admitting your mistakes, and asking for help, that softens you. Humility causes the wall we built around our hearts to crumble. It allows us to *love* again and receive love. When we can give love again and receive it, it will change our outlook on life. Life is much more precious with love in it. All of a sudden you will begin to value what you did not cherish in your previous season of life. Family will matter, healthy relationships with people around you will matter, and you will have *convictions* again. Conviction is a great thing; it is your best form of accountability — it is with you when others are not. It reminds you of right and wrong. This does not make you perfect, but when you fall short, humility fuels your conviction to help you make things right.

"Conviction is a great thing; it is your best form of accountability — it is with you when others are not."

The parties came and went. I remember going to one and telling two good friends of mine that I would be the designated driver (DD) because I was worried for them . . . *worried!* I had not felt worry in a long time. I went to one senior party and sat on a picnic table, way off to the side from where everyone was drinking and dancing, and talked with an old friend I had not hung out with in a while (probably because she had never really been a drinker or partier) and watched everyone get plastered. The drunker they got, the more they came over to me trying to get me to drink with them. I got every comment in the book: "Our senior year only happens once!", "You've changed so much—you need to be fun like you used to be!" and more. However, I refused. The more the comments came, the more irritated and stubborn I got. I did not stay long and talked my friends into leaving early with me. I realized I should not have gone, even being a DD. All it would take is one slip. That was the only one I went to, and the last.

Prom

I went to prom with a guy friend I had known since kindergarten. To be honest, I went for the opportunity to wear a pretty dress and get all beautified! We went to the dance for a couple hours, but then when everyone left to go party and check into hotels, I asked to go home. My friends could not believe it. Here it was, our senior prom, and everyone was going to stay in beautiful hotels and party all night, but all I wanted was to go home and be by myself! The guy I was with respected me, so he took me right home. My dad was shocked to see me return home only a few hours later. I realized I looked like a complete party pooper, and I was not used to that feeling, but I quickly remembered the nasty hotel rooms, people passed out, and the awful feelings I always had the next morning when I woke up and could not remember anything. A particular memory quickly flashed through my mind.

Earlier in my high school years, after one of the school dances, we all gathered at a friend's house. We were all drinking and doing drugs, like normal. As a few of us talked, we heard an argument going on outside between a drug dealer and one of my friends who had just started dealing. We walked outside to see what they were arguing about and the argument quickly escalated into a fight. As we watched them fight, hoping someone would break it up, the drug dealer (who was older), pulled out a knife and started stabbing my friend! Someone yelled, "Run!" My girlfriends and I ran to one girl's car and we drove off. We felt awful leaving the scene like that, but knew there was nothing we could have done, and we were terrified. We stayed on the phone all night with one of our guy friends who had taken our stabbed friend to the hospital, we were so concerned for him. Thankfully, he lived through it, though barely. We were worried about being witnesses that night. We did not know what that guy was capable of; after all, he had stabbed our friend right in front of us all! We did not sleep very well that night — to say the least. After remembering that night, quite frankly, I was happy to be in my own bed.

Love

My new life was off to an amazing start! I loved my parents again although I still went through many ups and downs with them. There was still a lot of attitude in me and I was use to always defending myself and taking care of myself. Coming back into a family environment after living that way is an extreme change mentally and emotionally. However, I hung out with my family a lot more, and had put all drugs, alcohol, stealing, clubbing, and illegal things behind me. The "feeling love" part was a very big thing for me. Though I could mention many more good things that changed in my life, my renewed ability to receive and give love was by far the biggest transformation in me.

I had so much hate and anger in me that it exhausted me to even try to suppress it. If my boyfriend cheated on me, I would make the other girl's life hell! At school on three consecutive days, I dumped Sobe juice over one girl's head. I also put gum in her hair at a football game, smashed an open sandwich in her face, and did anything I could think of to try and humiliate her, hoping to make myself feel better!

Once I made my cheating boyfriend drive me to the home of his ex-girlfriend and together, we egged her house with a huge Costco crate of eggs. We thought her parents were gone for the weekend, but apparently they had changed their minds, because about three quarters of the way through the crate of eggs, the girl's dad came running out, jumped on top of our car with his cell phone in hand, and said he was calling the police. I yelled at my boyfriend to take off, so he did, with the girl's dad hanging onto the car. He was banging on the windows for us to stop, but instead we sped up, then stopped short to try and knock him off the car. Still holding on, he jumped off (probably in fear for his life).

When I thought back on those moments I felt bad about them, embarrassed over what I had done. I could not believe that! It was as if my heart had suddenly grown two sizes, like the Grinch! I was now worried for others wanting to protect them and not hate them.

I remember apologizing to each family member for how I had acted toward them. I apologized to my brothers because I realized that my bad influence could greatly affect their future. I felt an extreme weight of guilt concerning them.

When I was a senior my brother, Scott, was a freshman. I remember hearing about something he had done that was pretty bad. I went into his room to confront him about it and he looked at me cross-eyed. He did not understand why I cared so much and knew very well my crazy reputation at school. I remember falling to my knees on his bedroom floor and crying, begging him not to follow in my ways and to stop whatever stuff he had already begun doing. I told him to learn from my mistakes and not to fall into the same stupid things I had. I remember him looking at me with confusion, telling me not to worry about him, but to simply worry about myself. My heart was broken for the right things, for morality, and for my brother. I finally wanted what was right for him, I finally felt concern for him. However, after a lifetime of beating him up, saying awful things to him, and being the worst example for him, he did not know how to respond to his now caring sister. That broke my heart worst of all. It was going to take time to repair all the deep wounds and important relationships I had ruined.

I asked my youngest brother to forgive me for how I had treated our mom and dad, and for being the worst role model as a sister. He responded, "You don't have to apologize! You're the best sister I could ever ask for! I love you, sis!" I teared up because I knew that was not true and could not believe my youngest brother had more love and wisdom in him than I did. He was an example to me that day. This reminded me of a scripture from the Bible, "Love covers a multitude of sins." (1 Peter 4:8) I felt covered . . . covered in grace.

Bandana Boy

Within a couple months of being off drugs, in the spring of my senior year, my mom and I went to a cycling class at the gym. After the class, dripping in sweat, we walked out the door to leave, when my mom stopped to talk with a young guy I did not think I knew. Before I could figure it out, my mom waved me over and said, "I want to introduce you to someone."

Oh no, I thought. *I'm going to kill her!* First of all, I had just gotten out of a cycling class, my face was as red as a cherry, my hair was slicked back in sweat, and I was wearing tight biking shorts! Second of all, I had not completely broken it off with Jack yet, though I was completely avoiding him at the time. Third of all, Western Washington University had accepted me, so I planned to attend in the fall to begin to pursue a degree in business. My plan was to start my own business and then get married in my late thirties. I did not need or want another boyfriend. I was so sick of guys after all I had been through and my trust level was at zero. However, I had no choice in that moment, so I walked up and shook the guy's hand. I noticed he was cute, but I really did not care at that point; I was done with males for a while. Then my mom went on to talk all about him, so I knew they had talked at least a few times. She then mentioned he was a youth pastor. Of course my mom had the biggest smile in the world as she told me that. As for me, I was ready to run! What was I going to say to him? For sure he would not want to talk to "my kind." So I quickly ended the conversation and told my mom I would wait for her in the truck.

Soon after, they both walked out of the gym and toward our truck together before he walked a different direction and waved goodbye to her and I. Just then I remembered she had pointed out this same guy to me the year before, in the gym. He was the guy that always wore basketball shorts and a bandana on his head.

"So what do you think of him?" my mom asked, interrupting my thoughts. "He's cute, huh?"

I said, "Yeah, mom, but you know I haven't broken it off with Jack yet, and I'm not sure if I'm ready for someone else yet—especially a youth pastor!"

"Who's Jack?" she replied sarcastically.

I said nothing. (She was right.)

"A youth pastor would be perfect for you," she mumbled.

A few weeks later, as I got out of my car to go in to work, I saw the same guy walking out the doors, toward me. *Oh no,* I thought. *It's him! What am I going to say? Why am I so nervous?*

He stopped in front of me and with a big smile on his face, said, "Hi! How are you?"

"Good, just on my way in to work," I said.

"I don't ever do this," he said, "but can I ask you for your number so we can talk sometime?"

I could not believe he had asked me that! I never game my number out—I had a boyfriend all through high school. But then I thought, *Oh, what the heck,* and gave him my number.

Clearly, my mom had not mentioned Jack to him! I walked inside with butterflies in my stomach. My boss (the one who had thrown himself on me), mentioned to me that the guy had asked him about me. I thought, *Oh goodness, if only he knew how weird my relationship with my boss had been!* I instantly felt overwhelmed with my life and intimidated by the life he lived. In my mind I pictured him living a perfect life, and I was so far from perfection! I mean, I definitely was not doing that great yet. If he actually called me, what was I going to say . . . to a pastor?

A couple nights later, my phone rang, I picked it up and saw it was him. *OMG!* I thought. I had butterflies in my stomach again. What was I going say to him? What was he going to say? I answered and said hello as if I did not know who it was.

He said, "Hi. This is Landon."

"Oh, hi!" I said.

We made small talk for a while and then completely got lost in our conversation. Two hours passed! I looked at my clock and could not believe it. I told him how long we had been talking and he said he had enjoyed every minute. I could sense he was being flirtatious, but I enjoyed it . . . for the first time. It felt different than when other guys had been that way with me. He was smooth, but not nasty (refreshing for sure!). Every smooth talker I had ever spoken to had one motivation—*sex!* I could sense this what not the case with him. There was nothing about him that made me feel unsafe. After we ended the call, I noticed how giddy I felt after talking to him. It was weird, to so quickly have such deep feelings for someone. I made myself back down.

We continued talking a couple times a week for hours and hours at a time. I convinced myself it was good to talk to him since he was a pastor and I could use the influence, coming out of the lifestyle I had been in so recently. As we talked more, I was shocked at how interested in me he was. I was not used to a guy caring so much about what I enjoyed in life and liked to do. Of course, I asked him questions about himself and what he did, but he never said too much about that. It was almost as if he knew that if he talked about all the ministry stuff too much, it might have overwhelmed me. I did not get most of what he said about it anyway. After all, I had gone to children's church as a kid, but then had taken five years off during my party stage, and had only resumed attending church just a few months before. So we just talked and laughed—we never wanted to get off the phone. I soon realized I could not help the way I felt about him.

Collision

One night, I was over at my dad's house, and had been talking with Landon on the phone for a while. Suddenly, I heard a loud knock at the front door. My dad answered it. The next thing I knew, my dad burst through my bedroom door telling me that Jack was at the front door and wanted to talk to me. I had not spoken to Jack in weeks! I told my dad I was on a really important phone call and to tell him I was not there. Well, Jack knew I was there because my car was parked out front, so my dad obnoxiously told him, "She told me to tell you she's not here."

Jack started crying and begged my dad to help him get me to talk to him. My dad came back into my room. Though Landon and I were still talking, he said, "Honey, I can't get him to leave! He's sitting on the couch crying. You have to talk to him. I can't do this for you!"

I was so irritated with Jack and his manipulative tears. There was no real sorry in him . . . for anything. The only thing he was ever sorry for was getting caught lying and cheating. Somehow, he would twist those situations and feel bad for himself. Why would I want to get off the phone with a guy who respected me and cared about me to talk with someone who had abused me for years? I told my dad to tell him to wait until I was off the phone.

Landon and I continued talking on the phone and I lost track of time and forgot all about Jack sitting out there waiting for me. My poor dad was doing his best to keep Jack occupied.

At some point, my bedroom door swung open and there was Jack, standing there. My dad had been unable to keep him out any longer. However, I was unwilling to get off the phone. I was still a strong personality — that never faded. If anything, that had actually grown stronger in me.

Landon asked what was going on, I told him a partial truth: an ex-boyfriend (though I had not completely broke up with him yet) was at the house and he wanted to talk with me, but I did not want to talk with him. Jack was questioning me at the same time, wanting to know who I was talking to; so I told him: a youth pastor. It was truthful and sounded completely innocent!

"Do I need to come over and help you?" Landon asked.

"No," I said, "I can definitely handle this."

Landon told me to keep him on the phone and he would wait, in case I needed him. So I left the phone on my bed and told Jack now was not the time for us to talk. It took me about ten minutes to convince him my conversation was innocent and that I would call him the next day, but I was not going to talk with him about anything right then. For me, it was about not letting him have control over me anymore. He had always held control in our relationship because I thought I was so in love with him and feared he would leave me. I had never before had the strength to leave him. His control over me that had allowed him to act however he wanted with no real consequences was over. I was taking back control and consequences were here, because I was done!

I finished my conversation with Landon that night and explained part of the history of my messed up relationship with Jack. I tried to keep it brief, though, because I felt it was still too soon to get into everything. The next day, I called Jack and tried to tell him it was over. He said he would drive to a cliff and the drive off it if I broke up with him. He screamed and cried and threatened to take his own life, trying desperately to pull on my heartstrings. He apologized up and down and promised he would change. I was trying to break up with him in the nicest way, using a soft voice, and even saying we could stay friends, but the moment I mentioned it was over, he became all the more irrational. Finally, I told him I was going to call his mom and tell her what he was threatening to do. I could not handle it on my own any more—and did not want to. I was so done!

I called Jack's mom and told her he was threatening suicide and somebody needed to go get him, but it was not going to be me. She said she would send his dad for him. I quickly called Jack back and told him his dad was on his way, hoping that would calm him down. Then I ended the call.

In that moment, I was so proud of myself for not bowing down to his control. Many times after that, Jack stopped by and tried to convince me we could make things work. Every time, I simply asked him to leave and always put the conversation off for another time. I was unable to handle his emotional ups and downs anymore. They had drained me and I disliked him more than ever, him and all his manipulative fits.

After a month of talking, Landon asked me out on a date. I said okay, but because I was so nervous about going on a date with a youth pastor, I cancelled. He asked me again. I said okay again . . . and then cancelled. Unwittingly, I was killing his pride. Still, he hoped the third time would be the charm. He asked me out again, but this time left eleven pink roses in my mailbox with a note that read, "I have a surprise for you—and your twelfth pink rose—if you would please go on a date with me tomorrow night." I called him, thanked him for the flowers, and told him I would go out with him. I knew I had to follow through that time. I melted over the roses and the note.

However, the night of our date, that nauseous feeling rose up in me again. This was for real. Was I really different? I realized this was deeper than a date for me, but symbolized if my change was *genuine* or not, because I refused to lead him on to believe I was someone I was not. In fact, right before he picked me up that night, my dad and I got into a big argument and were both screaming and cussing at one another. Not knowing Landon was at the front door, I paused, hoping he was not actually there, but then the doorbell rang. I felt sick and embarrassed, again.

I opened the door, trying to smile. "Is everything okay?" he asked. He was already getting a dose of my life, and this was me "making progress!" He was coming in during the growing pains season. I expected him to walk away, but to my surprise, he still wanted to take me out. So we walked out to the car and he opened my door for me. *Wow! He opened the door for me!* I definitely was not used to that! I looked down onto the seat and there was one pink rose, just like the note had said. I completely forgot everything that had just happened with my dad. I picked it up and got into the car. We pulled out of the driveway as he turned on some romantic music on low volume, so we could talk. He was definitely impressing me — on his A game for sure! That night, he took me to Seattle to a little Greek restaurant on Alki Beach with a gorgeous view of the water, a beautiful sunset, and a veggie pizza! Ha! It was a perfect night for me (and almost perfect for him, if there had been meat on the pizza).

During dinner, he asked question after question about my life. I felt as if I was in an interview, but I guess this was the real deal now and he needed to know who I was, or at least, what I had been through. Before he picked me up, I had made the decision that I was going to be completely up-front and honest with him about *everything* and answer every question he had, no matter how shameful I might feel. I did not want to be fake or have him like me based on a lie, so I told him everything. At many points, I remember waiting for him to get up and say, "Let's go," and announce the date was over. He never did. He had compassion for what I had been through and wanted to take care of me and protect me. Again, I was amazed by this response of love toward all my past behaviors and mistakes.

A few times he looked at me with a shocked expression as I told some of my stories, but I just kept going until I was completely finished telling him the majority of my story. When I was nearly finished, he interrupted me by grabbing my hands. He told me he really liked me and wanted to date me. He promised me that I would never again have to feel unprotected and ashamed like I had. He told me he was a virgin and planned on being a virgin until his wedding night, and that I would never have to worry about him disrespecting my body in any way. I did not even know what to say to that. I did not think a guy who lived like that even existed anymore! (He was the first I had met.) I completely melted . . . again!

After dinner, Landon took me down to the beach and we walked up and down the shore, talking about life and what we both wanted. When it got too cold, we headed back to his car. We both got in and he looked at me and said he was really serious about being with me and that he wanted a future with me. Again, I did not know what to say — it all seemed so quick. Though I still had trust issues, my heart beat differently when I was with him and talked with him. He was different.

When we got back to his car, he said he had to talk to me about something very important. I said, "Okay, what is it?"

"I don't want you to be mad at me or take this the wrong way," he answered.

"I think I have given you the majority of the shocking news tonight, so go ahead," I said with confidence that I would not be upset.

He told me that there was a girl at his church everyone (including her) thought he would marry, but he had taken her out on dates and tried to make it work and just knew inside she was not the one.

"Okay, and . . . ?"

He went on to tell me that he had not told her yet that she was not the one, and that she still believed he was. He paused, looking at me, I guess thinking I might cry or not want to be with him anymore.

"Phew! Me too!" I said.

"What?"

"You know that guy I told you was my ex-boyfriend, the one who has been awful to me?" I explained. "I haven't been able to totally break it off with him either because every time I try I feel manipulated!"

We sat in the car together that night, basically planning how to break up with our exes! We had similar situations, though his circumstance was definitely more "churchified" than mine, and mine was a bit more dramatic. Both of us needed the reason and strength to follow through with the thing we knew was right to do all along. Together we became each other's reason and strength.

That night when I got home I called my mom and told her that I was going to marry Landon! She reminded me it was close to midnight, she was very tired, and that she had only answered because she was worried I was calling that late.

"Good honey," she said sleepily. "But remember, you're only seventeen. But I'm happy for you . . . good night . . . it's midnight . . . good night."

"Mom, I'm really going to marry him!"

"We can talk more tomorrow, honey. Good night."

I did not care what time it was! I was not sleeping that night! I had gone from wanting to go to college to be a businesswoman who could not care less about marriage, to meeting my future husband! Landon called his dad that same night and told him I was going to be his wife. Neither of us knew we were going to say that to our parents, but we both knew we were going to marry one another.

My Fairy Tale

Our first date was on June 8, 2003, the day before my eighteenth birthday. My whole senior summer, I forgot about everybody from school and fell hard in love! He took me on the most fun and romantic dates all summer long. We went rock climbing, horseback riding, slid down water park slides, took long drives, and went to just about every romantic spot and restaurant in downtown Seattle.

One date in particular, I will never forget. He picked me up from my house and pretended we were going to rent a movie and watch it at his house. But when we arrived at his house, there on the couch was a beautiful black gown, heels, and jewelry he had picked out for me! He told me to go and get ready because he had a whole night of surprises planned for me. He borrowed his dad's old light blue '76 Impala, and we headed toward downtown Seattle. He took me to an amazing dinner spot on the water: white tablecloths, candlelight, and delicious food. Afterward, we pulled up to one of the most famous and oldest opera houses in Seattle, and big sign out front read, "Phantom of the Opera"! I had never been to anything like that. I was so excited!. We held hands the whole time. I did not know whether to pay full attention to the opera or think about how much I was falling in love with him—a love incomparable to my previous relationship! We had only dated for two months at the time, and what I felt for him was one of a kind, something I wanted for a lifetime.

After the opera, he said he wanted to take me to one more place. We walked to a tall building right next to the opera house. We took the elevator to the very top. He pulled out keys and opened a door to a condominium that belonged to his family. Rose petals and lit candles were everywhere! One of our favorite romantic songs was playing, "Kissing You," by Des'ree (from the movie *Romeo and Juliet*). He grabbed my hand and walked me over to the balcony and we danced on the top floor of this tower, overlooking Seattle, surrounded by the stars outside and the rose petals and candles inside.

Was I dreaming? I felt as if it could not really be happening to me. It was like a fairy tale. He had completely swept me off my feet! No one else existed, just he and I! Every time I was with him, he made me feel that way.

At my high school graduation, I remember just wanting to grab my diploma and run out of that place—happy to never return again! I did not go to any parties or out with any friends; I just wanted to be with Landon. I had made sure not to tell him about my graduation party, though. I did not think he was ready for all my family yet. However, halfway through the party, he showed up! I had no clue how he found out about it (mom must have invited him). Though I was so excited to see him, I was very nervous about him meeting my family and friends. Everybody loved him, of course, and my friends were very interested in finding out who this new guy was. They could not believe he was a youth pastor! They were shocked . . . and let him know they were shocked I was dating a youth pastor! I was stressed as they probed him with questions, but he laughed it off, putting me at ease again. I was so in love.

I started going to his church with him in downtown Seattle. I began to learn a lot of things about God I had never known before. First of all, his church felt like one of my old parties, but in church! It was crazy! People danced and shouted, ladies played tambourines . . . I loved it! I had always gone to quiet . . . well, to be honest . . . boring churches!

This church held my interest. However, the biggest thing for me was that I felt God's presence for the first time there.

Up to that time, I never knew you could talk with God and he would talk with you—or that you could feel him. I did not know much about the Holy Spirit. However, I started to learn, and as I was falling in love with Landon, I was also falling in love with Jesus! I had never felt that way about God before. The feeling was so intimate, so close, so intense. I felt love for God, appreciation for him, and wanted to get to know him more! I realized I had been having experiences with God for years, but never knew it was him! I realized, in a much bigger picture, how involved in our lives he is, how much he cares, and that he has an actual plan for us! I felt so much love around me, towards me, and for God! I could not wait to get to know him more!

One night, after one of our dates, we pulled up to my house and Landon asked me if I wanted to pray with him and ask God for the gift of tongues. I did not know what that was, so he explained to me what speaking in tongues was. I was freaked out by what I assumed it was and thought it was crazy. He explained to me that it was a language between a person and God, that it strengthened one's spirit man, and was normal, not a weird thing. I heard him out and enjoyed hearing about what it was, but was not so sure I was ready for it. I think I was even more nervous about praying for it and not getting it. I told him that I thought another time would be best . . . mainly out of fear. He told me he felt like it was time. He grabbed my hand and said we were going to pray together. I was so nervous! I did not want to pray in front of him! What if I sounded stupid or did not pray right? I had just started praying. He had been praying his whole life! I told him I did not know what to pray, so he told me what to say and that he would pray over me first, and after that, I could pray whatever was in my heart. He assured me there was no right or wrong way to pray.

Landon prayed for me and before I knew it, it was my turn. Did I mention I was *so* nervous? I was. I sat there quietly for a few moments and he lightly nudged me a "go ahead." Finally, I opened my mouth and began to ask God for the gift of tongues and for him to fill me with his presence. Landon started speaking in tongues in the background. I just waited and waited until all of a sudden, I felt a soft presence come over me, so I opened my mouth . . . and I started speaking in tongues! *OMG! What a rush! Who needs drugs with all this cool Jesus stuff?* I thought. I was so happy he had pushed me because I do not think I ever would have told him I was ready because I was fearful, but he saw it the whole time. After speaking in tongues for a few minutes, we both stopped and paused, just soaking up the soft peaceful presence that filled our car. I had never felt that kind of peace in my entire life. I had finally found it!

Sidenote: I have wondered why people are so open to drugs giving them a high, and weird, creepy visions, but think it is weird that God can give them visions, and so on. Is God not a "little better" than a drug? I do not understand this—and this is coming from someone who has been on both sides. Without the presence of God and the gift of speaking in tongues, I would not have made it to where I am today. They brought me true deliverance, strength when I needed it most, and kept me from running back to my old lifestyle when things got hard. If you want this gift in your life, you can pray right now, just like I did, asking God for this gift.

I put this in the perspective of being a parent. I would much rather have my kids in love with God and his presence than on drugs—even if I did not understand it! To push one's kids away from God has never made sense to me. I have found that those who push others from God have usually had a bad experience with a person who was a Christian (or claimed to be a Christian), and by so doing, let that person be God in their life. God is so much bigger than any person. People will always make mistakes, no matter *who* they are because they are *people*! They end up making a selfish decision and it turns others—sometimes their own kids and family members—from God who never did anything to hurt them! Bottom line: We cannot let people be God in our lives! Otherwise, we will always be disappointed. This is why *relationship* with God is so important! People often build relationships with people in the church, but when the people upset them or hurt them, they leave church and have a *screw God* mind-set. That makes no sense either. If I get in a fight with you and say hurtful things about you, you would not hate my mom . . . you would be upset with me. So do not take out on God your frustrations with people. Remember, God is the one who is fighting *for you*. He loves you like no person is capable of doing.

Now, there were other car rides with Landon that were not so . . . well . . . magical! I was still very early in my process of growth— everything did not change overnight! One day, we were on our way to pick up my brother from his friend's house. We were caught up in conversation when I realized I forgot to tell him to turn right about a mile back. I yelled, "Shit! Turn around. We passed it." I probably swore a hundred times a day, at least, before I met Landon. I had gotten much better since, but occasionally . . .they slipped out.

"Remember, God is the one who is fighting *for you*. He loves you like no person is capable of doing."

The car got silent; I looked over at him and asked what was the matter. He stared at me with this look like, *Really?*

I didn't get it. "What?"

"The mouth speaks what the heart is full of." he said, quoting Luke 6:45 from the Bible to me.

I sank down into my seat, saying under my breath, "Oops . . . sorry."

We both looked out our windows with grins on our faces; me mortified inside, and him probably laughing hysterically inside. I needed that accountability. After all, I desired change. It was like losing weight: I was trying hard but every once in a while, I would slip up and take a bite of cake! And Landon would be there to pull the rest of the cake away from me . . . and I would thank him for it later.

Because the truth was becoming more and more visible to me and my heart was softening, I had many unanswered questions. I could not understand how my dad had let me do all the things I had done without ever caring, or how now that I was attending church more than ever, I felt shame more than ever before! Because I was feeling and seeing more clearly, I was burdened with unanswered questions and working at new levels on purging generational curses out of me (things/issues passed down to me from my parents, grandparents, and others further back). Suddenly, I truly cared what others thought of me—not in an insecure way like before—I wanted a good reputation! I did not just want to forget my old life and jump into a new body to live a new life, I wanted to remember my past and never forget it so I would not lose my thanksgiving to God! I wanted the process of true change, not fake, false, or temporary changes. I was done with all of that. I had lived all the fake faces for a long time. I wanted to be real, the real me—the real me God intended when he created me! That was harder than I thought! So many church people, I found, wanted to hide their past or mistakes and look down on others for theirs.

Early on, I remember sitting on the front row when Landon preached. If he told us to turn to a certain book in the Bible (say Genesis), I would have to turn first to the table of contents to find where Genesis was. His friends and other leaders would look at me as I searched and laugh at me under their breath for not knowing. It seemed so silly since we all knew we were in there for the same reason, a *Savior*. We *all* needed saving!

A few months after I started dating Landon, I headed to college a couple hours north of where he lived. I was really emotional over leaving him, but I was excited about college. I was super nervous about being away from the security blanket of home and Landon. This was my test. I was away from him. Could I still stand? All the shame I felt about my past—could it heal? My frustration with my dad for allowing me so much freedom—could I forgive him? Was I ready for what was next?

CHAPTER 7
HEALING

A wise man once said, "Healing takes place in season, miracles happen in a moment." I had had my miracles: quitting drugs on the spot, being saved from countless close-to-death moments, supernatural encounters, and so on. I had experienced many miracles and was thankful for them. However, after the miracles, I needed inner healing. I wish the healing could have happened in a moment, but there was too much that had to be worked through, too many patterns and habits that had to be broken. I must say, submitting to the molding/healing process is the hardest thing you will ever do, but without a shadow of a doubt, the most rewarding thing you will ever do!

Once at college, I needed accountability! I was by myself with every temptation around me. Landon and I went from having our first kiss right before I left for school (very romantic by the way!), to him becoming my mentor. It was quite a switch, but I needed it. I was happy to have him in my life any way I could. He had me read books. My first assignment was *Good Morning, Holy Spirit*, by Benny Hinn. I loved it, and I loved learning. I found a young adult college group at a church close to campus to go to and tried to read my Bible every day. Landon visited me as much as he could, sometimes making the long drive up after a service just to take me out for a late cup of coffee and hand me some money for the week. Those were the moments I so looked forward to—him coming to visit me. But when he left, it was back to me fighting.

Side Note: Why do I say *fighting*? Anyone who has ever come out of a lifestyle like I did, or something hard, knows that to change that life pattern is a fight every day. Though it becomes a little easier over time, it takes self-discipline and a steadfast heart that refuses to give up. Giving up is so easy and so attractive sometimes. It seems weird that it would be, but it really is. Some days, running back to that old lifestyle that made you miserable suddenly appeals to you again, especially on the hard days. You must make an ultimatum with yourself that no matter what, *you will never give up!*

I was surrounded by things from my past and this was the first time I had to stand on my own— just three months after a major life change (six months after getting off drugs and alcohol). My roommate was crazy and partied all the time, which only reminded me why I did not do it anymore. I gave her two rules: 1) No parties in our room, and; 2) Never bring guys into our room, especially Jack, who attended the same college. Of course, only a couple months later, she ended up in a class with him and sat right next to him. Soon enough, she brought him over to our place. I walked in our room to see them standing there talking and laughing. I felt betrayed. The last thing I wanted him to know was where I lived! I gave my roommate a death glare, pulled her to the side and told her to get him out now, and then walked out and made my way to a coffee shop. I returned an hour later to confront her. I told Landon and he felt so frustrated because he had not been there by my side, but he was always there to encourage me.

It was always in my weak moments and on my hard days that temptation came. If Landon and I got into an argument or I got a bad grade on a test, temptation came—and it came hard! I often fought depression at college. It was getting harder and harder to live in the college atmosphere and be away from Landon, my family, and my church. I was a total loner because I was so nervous I would fall that I did not involve myself in anything at the school or make any friendships. I formed no life up there; my life was down south with my family and Landon. I was not a mature enough Christian to know how to set my own atmosphere (so to speak). I was afraid of failing and disappointing Landon and my family, but I felt so weak. I was beginning to learn that I could not find all my strength in Landon and our relationship; I needed to rely on my relationship with God.

In the spring of my freshman year at college, Landon drove up to visit me and told me his family was handing over their Seattle church and moving to Palm Springs, California. I obviously wanted to go with him. It was hard enough living a couple hours away from each other. I could not imagine living states away. I talked with my parents about it. They were extremely upset and did not want me to give up college. I knew I did not want to stay—not by myself. I could not stay. I was not strong enough. So after I finished out that year, I met Landon down in Palm Springs and moved my stuff down. I was so blinded by excitement I did not realize the hardest season of my life loomed before me.

Process

Moving to Palm Springs with Landon and his family was proof to us and everyone else that we were serious. I gave up a paid-for college education and family to be with him. We knew this was marriage preparation time, and we were going to be around each other more than ever. Any downfalls to our relationship or any bad side to us individually would surely show up (especially mine)!

After the excitement of the move ended, Landon stepped into position as my mentor more than ever before, and now it was 24/7. I was living with a pastor's family, and I felt as if I was under extreme pressure. I was afraid I would disappoint or embarrass him. I was worried I was not what his parents wanted for their son. In our first three months, when we were falling in love, nobody and nothing else mattered. Then I went off to school and we had different lives with different people. Now we were back together for the first time in a long time, but we were also joined by his family, did church stuff constantly, and were in the thick of marriage preparation all at the same time.

I started freaking out, questioning what I was doing there. I felt like a fake. *What was I doing, living with a pastor's family and dating a pastor?* I loved God and was confident of that, but I was not confident in my "Christianity." For example, the family would have prayer on Tuesday nights, and his dad would call on me to pray out loud in front of them. I did not want to pray in front of them! I did not know what to say. In their defense, I do not think they knew anything that was going on inside of me, but I was humiliated! I just wanted to run again! I felt as if everything I said and did was on display and might be judged.

After only a few months of living in California, I was depressed, even though I had Landon with me. One night, I could not handle the pressure anymore, so I started packing my bags to go home. Landon came in to ask me what I was doing.

"I'm going home! I cannot handle this anymore!" I yelled in response.

"You can't just run from all your problems all the time! You need to face them and deal with them!"

"No, I can't! You just don't understand! I don't fit here!" I had to go home. I kept stuffing everything in my suitcases.

He finally grabbed my arms and yelled at me, "Stop! Stop packing right now and talk to me! Stop for a second and think about what you're doing!"

But I was too ashamed. I felt so humiliated, so little. I could not live like that anymore! I did not fit! I was trying to be better but I did not feel like I was good enough. I did not care at that moment, I just wanted out! I shoved his arms away from me and kept packing. I began to cry. I was breaking down. Landon grabbed me and pulled me away from the bags, trying to get me to stop so he could talk to me. He assured me that everything would be okay, but that I could not quit because I had come too far to give up now. He told me he loved me and was willing to do whatever it took to help me… but I did not know how to help me.

I finally calmed down and cried in his arms. He started talking to me about generational curses and things that are passed down to us from our parents that had been passed down to them from their parents that sometimes go back many generations. I was faced with my own inner demons. They had to be dealt with, or I risked passing down to my children. I knew for sure I did not want that!

I told him that I was willing to let my guard down to let him in to tell me what I needed to change. Because of my past, I was so used to making all my own decisions for myself and fighting for my life constantly, that once again, I was faced with having to give up control! However, I realized this time around it was best for me. Even though I put up a fight again, it was shorter-lived and less violent! Ha! I was making progress! There were no cops involved this time, just my boyfriend having to restrain me. I was thankful for his persistence in helping me and loving me through all my rough times. The hard part was trying to figure out what the root issues were for me. I did not understand what roots were and where my negative emotions and depression were coming from. I couldn't keep trying to control the outer issues; I needed to rip out the roots!

"I couldn't keep trying to control the outer issues; I needed to rip out the roots!"

One night, Landon took me on a date to Los Angeles, about a two-hour drive away. On our way home we got into an argument. My game was the silent treatment—a control tactic—but I felt so right about doing it, I did it. For a solid hour, I did not say a word. He tried every way possible to get me to talk—good and bad. Of course, I paid no attention to the good ways and used the bad ways as more fuel to punish him with silence. Finally, he pulled over on the side of the freeway, put the car in park, and turned it off. I looked at him in disbelief, committed to not breaking my silence. I crossed my arms and looked out the window with my back to him. He made himself comfortable and said we were not going anywhere until I stopped my childish ways and talked to him. After ten minutes, I finally shouted, "Take me home . . . *now!*"

He did not flinch, but simply said, "Are you going to talk to me now?"

I had already broken the silent treatment and, to be quite honest, I was sick of my own game. "What exactly do you want to talk about?" I said haughtily.

"Well, two things," he answered. "First . . . what happened tonight? Second, I would like to talk about how you are acting right now . . . and for the last hour and a half! How are we going to communicate in our marriage if my wife gives me the silent treatment? How am I going to help like you said you would let me, if you refuse to talk to me about what's going on? You have to let me point out weaknesses and trust me enough that I'm not saying them to hurt you, but to help you."

As I listened to his speech I slowly softened, but still tried to hold onto some of my stupid pride. I think I answered back something ridiculous to try to spin some of it onto him, so I did not have to take the whole brunt of the situation. He immediately apologized. Then I really felt stupid. I told him I was sorry too.

"Now that we got that out of the way, let's talk," he said.

I was nervous. He started to talk to me about letting go of control, stubbornness, manipulation, and more. Oh boy, I had so many things to work on! In fact, that was the next year of my life: breaking thought processes down, learning why I responded certain ways, and so on. But the biggest one of all was my shame. He did not know I was struggling with it as deep as I was, but I did not know either! Shame was the biggest battle of the first five years of my new life. I did not want to speak in front of others, pray in front of anybody, or talk about my past to anyone. I felt ashamed of my own family as if they were a part of my old life. My relationship with my family grew more distant.

I did not know exactly what was going on, but I felt no value and so far away from the perfect Christian/pastor's wife image that I felt I had to live up to. However, I would always come back to how much I loved Landon. I reminded myself of our beginning dating days, knowing that I was supposed to marry him. I had to stop questioning it and lay down my pride in this awful process.

Commitment

Eight months into living in California, Landon proposed to me! One thing we both knew for sure was how in love we were. He surprised me right after Christmas. He flew up to Seattle and asked me to look out the window of my mom's house. There he was, standing in the front yard, waving at me! I had not seen him for two weeks, so I was so excited! I thought this was the surprise, his visit, but a couple nights later was New Years Eve, December 31, 2004, and he had a bigger surprise planned for that evening. He took me shopping for a new outfit that day and told me we were going out on a date that night in Seattle. We had lived in California for a while, so I was very excited about our plans in downtown Seattle, since that is where we first started dating.

He started the date by taking me to our favorite steak restaurant, Morton's the Steakhouse. While we talked I noticed him sweating a little bit and looking all around, acting fidgety. He was so nervous! I kept asking him if he felt okay. He assured me he was feeling great. At the end of the meal, he got up to go to the bathroom. As I waited at the table, I noticed everyone was staring at me. I worried that food might be stuck in my teeth or something. Staff kept walking by and complimenting me.. *Hmm*, I thought. *This is weird. Maybe they think I am someone I am not.*

Then I realized Landon had been in the bathroom for a while. I began to worry, thinking he was sick and just did not want to tell me because he did not want to ruin our date. I had just called a waiter over to ask him to check on Landon when he came out of the bathroom with a big smile on his face. I looked at him funny and asked, "Are you sure you're okay?"

"I'm great!" he responded as he paid for the bill.

When we started toward the door to leave, everyone waved and said goodbye. *How strange*, I thought again.

Landon then took me to all the different lookouts that surrounded Seattle. I realized he was taking me to all the same places he had taken me on our first date, starting with the same lookout and ending at the same cliff, right above Alki Beach. We made it to the final spot just ten minutes before midnight! Landon and I stood on the edge of the cliff, looking over the gorgeous city of Seattle and the Puget Sound. He stood behind me with his arms around me, talking in my ear about the rest of our lives and how much he loved me. Then everyone started shouting, "10 . . . 9 . . . 8 . . . ," and all of a sudden Landon turned me around to face him, took the L ring off me I had worn the entire time we dated, and threw it over the cliff! I looked at him with disbelief, thinking, *What are you doing?*

When I looked back at him, he was on one knee. He began proposing to me and asked me to spend the rest of my life with him. I looked down at my hand as he put a gorgeous ring on my finger! I was in shock. Call me gullible, but I had no idea at all that Landon intended to propose that night. I thought it would be at least another six months before that would happen. I said yes of course, and while everyone cheered and celebrated, fireworks went off and he spun me around. I had forgotten about everyone around us until they all started clapping for us. We just held each other. I was completely surprised and could not let go of him. He finally let go of me to ask what I thought of the ring. (I had not even really looked at it yet!) I looked down at it. It was gorgeous! Honestly, I could not believe it. He explained that he had ordered the ring specially designed for me—a one-of-a-kind ring.

Wow! I was only a nineteen-year-old girl, off of drugs for just one and one-half years, standing there with my prince charming, with a promise of marriage on my hand! How could this happen to me? (I asked myself that question often.) And how had it all happened so quickly?

Part of me felt as if this must all be a mistake. Had I portrayed someone other than myself—and had he actually fallen in love with her, not me? I just did not feel that all these wonderful things could happen to me after all the bad I had done! Stealing, drinking, drugs, hatred, fighting, anger, jealousy, sex outside of marriage . . . to then be swept off my feet? On the other hand, I loved every moment of my new life. I felt *valued* for the first time in a long time. He made me feel like a princess.

I remember living with the awful fear that at any moment, the fairy tale I was living would be ripped away from me, and I would awaken in my reality—a nightmare life. My life before had been so dark, awful, and depressing, it still haunted me at times. I had lived the life I wanted. I had fought and left my family for it. I had thought I was having the time of my life and lived it up. How could I have been so deceived? I had fallen in love with a false pleasurable existence. What kind of pleasure was there in having sex when I did not want it? What was pleasurable about being hung over? How fun was it to be left to die alone in an abandoned apartment by a "friend"? Where was the fun in fighting men off me as they tried to rape me . . . or worse yet, finding my best friend after she had been raped by three guys? Where was all the pleasure I had convinced myself I would find in that life? There was none, because if there was, I would have been the one to find it! I fought hard for that life, and got nothing back but pain and a broken heart. So how was it that I was standing on a beautiful lookout, on New Year's Eve night, fireworks going off, in the arms of the man who surpassed any dreams I ever had . . . who had made a life promise to me? How could this happen to me?

We were engaged for seven months and married on July 16, 2005. I was twenty years old and he was twenty-two. We were still babies. We waited to have sex until our wedding night, and it was worth it! The next day, we flew out to a small peninsula off the coast of Puerto Vallarta, Mexico. We stayed in a beautiful house off a small cobblestone pathway, with only four other homes around us. When we looked out over our deck we saw gorgeous water all around us. We woke up to cooked breakfast served upstairs on the patio, where a beautiful breeze blew. I was with the man of my dreams. I still could not believe this was my life.

Face 2 Face

When we got back from our honeymoon, we packed our things to move to Columbus, Ohio, to a large church that had hired us to serve as youth pastors. Landon surprised me by buying a new and fairly large house (for our first house), and it was close to the church! This would be my first true experience as a pastor's wife in ministry. It was bittersweet. I was so excited to start married life with my husband, but I had moved even further from my family in Seattle. I was also nervous about ministry, but convinced myself I would be the supportive wife for my husband. When we were dating, Landon told me he did not care if I served in ministry or not, he just wanted me to be his wife. I always felt safe and assured in that statement. But somehow this changed when we moved to Columbus, Ohio.

We got thrown in deep and quick—at least it felt that way to me. The week we arrived we got a call that our pastor wanted to take us to the Bahamas with him on a preaching engagement. We had not even unpacked our house yet when we started packing suitcases for the trip! We traveled with our pastor a lot while building the youth ministry.

The youth ministry had taken a major hit just before we arrived, and it would require a lot of time and effort to get built back up again. Landon came to me and told me I needed to start a ministry for girls. I replied, "No way!" He told me that he felt I was supposed to, so I needed to start planning for it. I put everything I had ever read or heard about submission on the back burner in that moment. I told him there was zero chance of me doing that. I had nothing to say and no idea how to even start it or what to do with it. I had never had a real mentor (other than Landon), youth pastor, big sister—no one. I had no example of what I needed to be to them, or what I needed to say to them. I was still in the honeymoon stage. I mean, we had only been married for a month! But it was being ripped away—fast!

Since Landon would not let the idea go and I felt a little convicted about it, I finally convinced myself I would try the Bible study thing out one night, thinking only five girls would show up. I planned to talk for a few minutes one night with a couple girls, and then hang out. I thought I could surely come up with something to say for a few minutes. I still was not sure if it was God's idea, the devil's . . . or even Landon's stupid idea. Surely it was not a good idea.

The night came. I showed up with some notes scribbled on a sheet of lined notebook paper folded up in my Bible. I still hoped someone would save me from this. I walked into the room a couple minutes late, trying to stall. When I peeked around the corner I saw thirty girls and some young adult women leaders waiting for me! I nearly had a heart attack! I had convinced myself the only way I would do it is if there were a few girls there, not thirty plus! *Holy crap!* (Literally.) What was I going to do? I had nothing to say to them! Seriously, what would I say? I had been saved for less time than the majority of the girls sitting in there had! Oh my! I felt like running again. It definitely crossed my mind. I was literally tempted to run!

As I leaned up against the wall around the corner trying to figure out what I was going to do, I heard "the voice" again: *Heather, stop making this about you! This is not about you! It is about these girls who need someone to love them! Just be there for them like you needed someone when you were their age.* Whoa! I had totally "got told"! I needed that. It erased all the fear that bound me up and brought me true perspective. This had nothing to do with how I was going to sound, but everything to do with being there for those girls. I walked in and said hi to them and sat in the chair set up for me. I straightened up and began to tell them about me. After that, I cannot recall what I said, but by the end of our time we were all hugging and crying on each other's shoulders! It was amazing. It was the best feeling to be to the person for these girls that I had so wished someone had been to me. I had ministered to someone else for the first time. It was an amazing feeling. I fell in love with those girls quick! I called them "my girls."

I ended up turning that Bible study into a sorority style girl's ministry, with rush weeks every couple of months where we did crazy things. One time, they had to do a full night of hilarious things wearing blindfolds. At the end of the night, all the girl youth leaders drove all the girls out to a ranch where they had to roll around in horse manure! Some of them freaked out, worried about ruining their hair, but to their surprise, I jumped in at the end and all of us laughed hysterically. One girl rubbed it all in my hair — something I will never forget. This got us a lot of attention in the church — good and bad! We were definitely nuts! That is exactly how I wanted it. For me to do this, it had to be enjoyable and I had to be me.

The girls did Celtic dancing for the whole youth church and even in a local mall — solos and all that they had to choreograph! We ordered shirts and sweatshirts with the slogan, "Girl's Gone Holy!" We had all the fun but without anything nasty. I learned the girls really needed it all because many of them had lived the kind of life I had! They came from rougher neighborhoods than I had. They were experimenting with a lot of the same things I had.. A few of the girls wanted nothing to do with me in the beginning, calling me "Barbie Doll," thinking I had everything made for me in life. I sat down with two of the leaders of that little rebellious group and told them my testimony — the first time I had told it all. Their jaws dropped lower and lower as I shared. Their countenance and tone changed dramatically. "Ms. Heather, we had no idea!" they said. "We thought you wouldn't understand anything we were going through. You look perfect and like you have had everything handed to you."

I realized for the first time how my past could be used as a strength. It built unity and trust with these girls. I had something in common with them. In fact, I became like Mama Bear with them, fiercely protective toward guys who tried to hit on them, abusive parents, or anyone who tried to mess with them. I taught them how to set boundaries and cling to purity. I showed them how to dress with dignity, speak with grace, and emphasized that ultimately, their loyalty was always to be God first. We called it F2F (Face to Face), based on the scripture where Moses spoke with God face to face. I wanted these girls to seek the face of God and relationship with him.

"I realized for the first time how my past could be used as a strength."

One of the girls that had been part of that rebellious group I told my story to was named Sheree`. One day, after losing someone close to her, Sheree` flipped out. I tried to counsel her, but there was no calming her down. She was hysterical and said she wanted to kill herself. After I finally got her calmed down a little bit (or so I thought), I told her I would bring her home. Landon and I got her into our car and started following her older sister to their home, which happened to be in the ghetto. In fact, I had never been in a neighborhood like it before. It was completely run by gangs and no one entered or left without knowledge of those who "ran" it. Let me just say, Landon and I stuck out like sore thumbs! People in every car that passed stared us down.

We stopped at a stop sign and suddenly, Sheree` jumped out of our car threw herself down right in the middle of the street! I jumped out of the car and tried to pull her up and out of the road. She was a lot bigger than I was, so she was winning. She screamed that she did not want to live anymore and to leave her alone. She yelled at Landon to get me and leave the neighborhood. I thought she was saying that so I would leave her alone. Little did I know, we were not "allowed" in that neighborhood, and by her causing a scene, kicking and screaming at a white girl (me!), the picture of me yelling back at her and trying to get her into our car did not look good! My adrenaline kicked into high gear and I got pissed. I started yelling at her sister to come help me get her out of the road, but she was across the street and unable to cross due to passing cars. As all this went on, cars slowed down and their occupants looked at us as if we were the problem.

"Go help Landon!" Sheree` shouted. She jumped up and I turned around to see a car packed with thugs pulling up next to my husband's car. Sheree˅ and I ran to our car. Sheree˅ talked to them and told them everything was okay, and to leave us alone. As I walked up to their car, Landon yelled at me to get back into our car. The driver of the other car told us we had about one minute to get out of "their" neighborhood. Still filled with adrenaline, I yelled, "Get away from our car, right now!"

Landon gave me a death glare and pointed at the front seat for me to get in immediately. Sheree˅ had a look of disbelief on her face after I yelled. I got in our car and we drove away. When we got out of the neighborhood, Landon let me have it! I had not realized how volatile a situation we had gotten ourselves into at the moment, but that day I realized how much I loved those girls. I felt the "momma bear feeling" in a big way that day. Though I was not a mother at the time, I experienced how far love will go.

The girls ministry kept growing and growing until seventy-five girls were part of it. We ran a lot of the youth ministry: events, skits, worship, outreach, and more. I can truly say they were the heartbeat of that youth ministry, and they became mine too. We did all kinds of fun things; sleepovers at my house, Christmas caroling, waterslides, and more. We also had nights where everyone would openly talk about everything they had been through, and then pray over each other. Sometimes we would get so lost in ministering to one another that what was supposed to be an hour-long meeting would run three hours long! I loved watching them grow and get stronger. It was a privilege for me to get to experience that with them.

I always encouraged the girls in their *purity*. This was one of my main messages to them. It may seem funny for a girl who had come out of a lifestyle that was anything but pure to be teaching it to them, but I valued what I had not had while growing up, and I wanted them to have it for themselves. The message was in my heart, so I could not stop sharing it with them. I wanted more for them—more then what I had settled for at their age. Many of them really listened, and I watched their lives change dramatically because of it. They put their teenage attitude to good use and refused anything less then what God had for them. I loved it!

When we first moved to Columbus, some of the girls were having sex in the church bathrooms before or after service. A year into

F2F, the same girls were ditching their boyfriends and telling them they needed to be a man of God before they would be allowed the privilege of dating them! They grew this pure confidence that was contagious . . . even to me. They probably thought it came from me, but they were changing me. My heart was changing.

I started stepping out a little more, doing a little more during services, ministering and encouraging the youth church. I was falling in love with broken young people and watching the restoration process in their lives! I shared my testimony a couple times. As I did, I could feel the shame melting away. When you refuse to hide your past, it cannot control you anymore. I learned that bringing the awful things you have done to light will completely free you!

"When you refuse to hide your past, it cannot control you anymore."

Breaking Shame

Our church held a big conference attended by thousands of people from all over. We led the youth service. At our service, praise and worship was amazing. As I sang and lifted my hands, out of nowhere, I heard "the voice" give me an offering word (an offering word is a short teaching on giving directed to the congregation before people give.) I thought that was so strange since I had never taken an offering before. About ten seconds later, Landon leaned over to me and told me to take the offering after worship. My stomach instantly soured as I looked around at the thousands of people crammed into the service. *No way!* I thought.

I leaned over and told Landon, "No way."

He responded, "I am not asking you . . . . I am telling you to do it."

"I'm not doing it," I said.

He assured me again that he really felt I was supposed to take the offering and to think about it for another minute. I knew I had already heard what I was supposed to say, but was full of fear! As I sat thinking, all I could hear were thousands of people singing behind me. I became paralyzed with fear. I leaned over and whispered in Landon's ear, "I'm not going to do it."

He sighed with disappointment and went up a couple minutes later and did what I knew I was supposed to have done. As he spoke, I was instantly filled with deep regret. I could not shake it all evening. I remember crying myself to sleep that night, not because I felt I had let my husband down, but because I felt I had let God down. I realized in that moment, God was first in my life. At some point, he became more important to me than anyone or anything. I knew it when I felt the deepest amount of disappointment I had ever felt, disobeying God.

Sidenote: I think this is why so many people deny God. They do not want to deal with the feeling of disappointing him. If you do not believe, the pressure of following through is not there, so you think, *Oh well.* You make a mistake and think, *Oh well.* You do whatever you want and think, *Oh well.* But the truth is, you are missing the *freedom* factor, without God. I realized shame and disappointment do not come from him, they come from myself and Satan. "The thief (Satan) comes only to steal and kill and destroy. I (Jesus) came that they may have life and have it abundantly." (John 10:10) When we call on him, he forgives our mistakes and sets us free from our sin! His love and grace cover us when we receive him as our Savior! You don't have to live a perfect life, you just have to live for the perfect one, Jesus. He will use your imperfections to glorify himself and set others free. Only Jesus can do that! Conviction is healthy; condemnation is not. Jesus does not condemn, he beings freedom!

I remember asking Him to forgive me that night. Actually, I unnecessarily asked him to forgive me over and over the next week until I actually felt him smile at me and whisper, "You don't have to ask anymore. Once was enough."

I remember promising him I would never knowingly disobey him again, no matter how hard or scary the task! I found out the feeling of disappointing him actually arose from a heart that wanted to please him. He did not expect me to be perfect, so I needed to forgive myself, which is usually the hardest task. I forgave myself and felt joy to move on with no shame attached. I told Landon what happened and he smiled at me and said he would help keep me accountable (*gulp*). Now it was up to me to keep my end of the bargain. After all, it was my promise. I was actually internally excited about it. Throughout this whole little situation, I had unknowingly formed a trusting bond with God. I knew he would catch me before I fell. You may not always know what he has for you, but when you form a real relationship with him, there is this weird security in which you just know that you know that you know he will be there. I was truly experiencing new levels of freedom!

The war against shame stormed on. What a process! Even though I was growing fast, I still had to deal with many things. I had self-image issues, fears, and insecurities, yet was all the while ministering to the girls about self-image, fear, and insecurity. I felt hypocritical sometimes, but then I would feel an overwhelming, encouraging presence come over me. How was I to genuinely get through these things without walking them out? After all, that was what I was doing. I was fighting daily to be the best example I could be for the girls. It was the best accountability ever! I did not want to let those girls down like so many others had. My personal prayer life began to grow and my hunger to know the Bible increased immensely. I knew that the more Bible in me, the quicker the change would be in me. I knew this was true because I saw it happening in my life and in the girls' lives.

Landon and I served that church for a couple years until we felt we were supposed to move on. Leaving there was one of the hardest things I have ever done, but some of my best ministry memories come from our time with that youth group. I will never forget F2F. They marked me.

We moved back to the eastern side of Washington state, Spokane, where Landon's family was pastoring a church. I was nervous, but excited about the move. All of our family was finally in the same state, but I was a different person. I had changed so much in Ohio that I was unsure how to act with our family, especially in ministry. I realized I was still carrying shame and was trying to seek approval. In Spokane this became more obvious than ever before. Landon and I enjoyed building the youth ministry and traveling together. (We ministered on the road at conferences, camps, and special services.) One day he came to me and said, "Everywhere we go, I want you to open up before I preach and share your testimony." (A testimony is your story of redemption—how you were renewed and set free from whatever held you in bondage.) I was very nervous about this, but was quickly reminded of the promise I made God. "Okay, I'll do it," I answered.

We traveled quite a bit, and every time I opened with my testimony. An incredible power filled the room every time I told my story—young people were crying everywhere. Sometimes I would have an altar call and pray over the young people individually. Other times, I would pray over them as a group. It always amazed me that though I was telling these young people about my deepest, darkest, and most shameful moments and it was helping them! My mistakes and sin and how God set me free were bringing freedom to them through God's power! Amazing! God used my past sin to set others free from theirs—only God could spin that one!

I started speaking at churches when we traveled, and when we took our youth group to Mexico on mission trips. The mission trips were truly life-changing for me. On those trips, I found out I had a huge passion for other nations. There were no boundaries to helping others on mission trips, which I loved! We helped prepare and set up an orphanage. We went into villages and did small performances that glorified Jesus and communicated his gospel. I got to witness miracles happening in peoples' bodies as we prayed for them..

We went into one hospital where uninsured people with no money for medical care were literally left to suffer and/or die from easily curable sicknesses and recoverable injuries. As we walked in, I looked over at our team and saw they looked freaked out. The hospital had packed suffering people into small rooms. They had tied up broken legs with rope instead of slings. They had wrapped broken arms in gauze and tape instead of casts. Malnourished babies barely clung to life.

Out of the blue, I felt a boldness come over me. I pulled our team into a corner and said, "We're not just here to watch and visit these people. We must pray for them! You don't need any specific prayer, just ask God to heal them and God will do the miracle. Do not be afraid: You are not healing them—God is. Just be willing to pray!" With that, they all went out and started praying.

Miracles started happening all around us. People were freaking out because they did not know what was happening, so they were calling in nurses from everywhere. The majority of our team members could not understand what they were saying because they did not speak Spanish. We spoke English and only a few of us had translators. My translator ran over to me and told me the nurses and family members of the patients wanted to know what our kids had said and what had happened because so many patients' pain and sickness had gone!

I remember one man whose horse had bucked him off a few days before, causing him to hit his head on a rock. He had been in a coma ever since. His cousin had sat there with him all three days, hoping he would respond to someone in some way. We started to pray with him, when suddenly, his eyes opened, he bolted forward and sat upright in his bed, and looked around the room! His cousin started yelling, "What's happening? What's happening?" (in Spanish). I told my translator to explain who Christ was, that he had died on the cross for our sins, and could heal our bodies. The cousin of the guy who had been in a coma started crying. He thanked us over and over. We asked him if he wanted to ask Jesus into his heart and accept him as his Lord and Savior. He said yes! We led him in that simple prayer and God did the rest.

This happened over and over until the head doctor came over to us and asked to speak with me. I thought we might be in trouble and asked to leave, but that was not the case. He wanted to know what was healing people and if I could explain it to all the doctors and nurses in the hospital. I told him I could (of course). I walked into a large back room where all the doctors and nurses in the hospital waited to hear from me! I felt more than honored, but truly humbled as well. Here were these faithful servants, working in a hospital no one wanted to work in (much less enter) — educated people — who wanted to hear about our great God! I was up for the task.

I brought my translator in with me and told her to start speaking in tongues. (I did not even think that might seem weird to them because it had become so normal for me.) There we were, my translator and I, speaking in tongues as a room full of doctors and nurses listened to us. None of them knew what we were doing. I stopped and explained to them what speaking in tongues was, and told them that if they wanted that, all they had to do was ask the God I was about to tell them about, and he would give them that gift. I told them all about Jesus and his miracles. At the end, I led them in prayer and they all repeated after me, asking Christ into their hearts! It was an amazing day. One I will never forget. We made many trips to Mexico the three years we lived in Spokane.

On another mission trip, shame was broken off of my life forever. My husband and I were going to speak at a youth camp at our mission church in Tepic, Nayarit. They had scheduled me to speak at one of the morning services and I felt strongly I was to speak about *shame*. At first, I was worried that I just wanted to speak on shame because it was something I dealt with. But every time I doubted this, the feeling that I should speak on it was only magnified. I had the overwhelming belief that the service was going to be powerful. I had no idea it was going to unlock something in me too!

The night before I was scheduled to preach, I was nervous — more of an anxious nervous. I felt ready. I had confidence that God was going to use me. Also, my topic was personal. I wanted other people to be set free from shame so they could go out and do all the things God called them to do. While studying the Bible I had learned that shame started in the beginning, in Genesis, with Adam and Eve. The majority of us know the story of Adam and Eve, the first two people God created on this planet. God gave Adam and Eve freedom to oversee all creation and reap the benefits of all God had made except one thing in the Garden of Eden: the tree of the knowledge of good and evil. A serpent came and tempted them by putting deception in them, saying, "Did God really say . . . ?" They listened and allowed the serpent to put seeds of selfish desire and impurity in them. This led to Adam and Eve giving in to the temptation to eat fruit from the forbidden tree. They sinned against God. The Lord spoke to them, questioning them about what they had done. They soon realized they were naked and covered themselves with leaves. They *ran* to try and *hide* from God though he called out to them and walked in after them. *Hmm, they sinned, God went after them, they ran and hid . . .* this sounded familiar.

I had heard this story many times, but reading it this time was different. It was as if the words on the page were pop-ups like those in children's books. The letters stood out so vividly: **"RAN"** and

"HID," and "COVERED THEMSELVES." This is what I had done for years! It starts with disobeying God, which then leads to the mistake/sin. This leads to separation from God (running and hiding) and ultimately, *shame* (covering ourselves). I learned that *we* separate ourselves from God! He never runs from us or pushes us away. *We* run from him! In fact, when we fall short/sin, he comes after us!

We have been deceived to believe that if we sin, God no longer wants anything to do with us, so we have to run from him. All the while, he calls out to us. I realized I had allowed the serpent's voice to be louder in my ear than God's for way too long. It is important to note here: The serpent's voice can come through a person. It can speak through people we love, friends, family members, teachers, professors, whoever!. No matter where the serpent's voice comes from, we must deny it and listen for God's voice. He will speak to you. He will come to you if you do not run from him!

"We have been deceived to believe that if we sin, God no longer wants anything to do with us, so we have to run from him."

Shame has been a tool of the devil's since the beginning of time to deceive people. It can make us think we want something that is not good for us (at least that we knew at one time was not good for us), but suddenly think is okay for us. Hello! That captured my whole past. I had been so deceived! The whole time I lived that way, I did not know there was a demonic influence leading me into the darkness I experienced. I thought it was all me! I mean, I did make all the decisions, but I was clearly being led by the wrong influence. Of course, when you are the one in it, it is not so clear. The crazy thing is, once we fall for the temptation, we think we will feel better — all the while piling shame upon more and more shame. This is why so many people (including me), attempt suicide. (Sadly, too many accomplish it.) I was not happy, but I thought I was choosing the "fun life," though I never experienced joy or peace. It was not until I surrendered my life to God that I experienced those things and came to live in them daily. I could not wait to release what I found out about shame — it was already changing my life!

The next morning, I woke up and got ready. I prayed all morning. I grabbed my notes and Bible and went to the service. I remember worship being awesome that morning . . . and I felt so ready! When I grabbed the microphone I let them know it was not going to be a normal note-taking service, and that that they needed to open their hearts. I knew God was going to do "heart surgery" on many of the young people. I began to preach and the power of God filled the place. I remember looking into so many of those kids' faces, and as tears streamed down their cheeks, I knew the message was hitting them. I gave the altar call for those who wanted shame broken off of their lives, and just about every single young person came to the front! I started praying over them and we all felt the amazing presence of God. The rest of the week I heard testimony after testimony of how God had healed hearts and broken shame off of lives (after all, that was the title of my sermon, "Breaking Shame").

I felt so free — free to talk about my past, free to minister . . . free from shame! I remember Landon telling me that day that he did not have to preach the rest of the week — I should! I took that as a great compliment, coming from my husband, as I think he is the greatest preacher ever. After God, Landon had made it possible for me to preach that sermon. He had never given up on me when I tried. He sat in the front row cheering me on as I stood up front cheering on a couple hundred teenagers! My passion was young people. Wherever I was, I was going to encourage them to dream bigger, live purer, and do all that God had called them to do. I was living proof, after all, that no matter what you have done or where you have been, God *can* and *wants* to use you. If you let him, he will blow your mind!

CHAPTER 8
LIFE NOW

My life now is indescribable! It is indescribable because my thanks-giving to God has no end to it. When I go to thank him, I do not know where to start and where to end. This is nearly an impossible task but the most necessary one of all. My life's mission is to tell as many people as I can about the goodness of God, that he is most definitely real, and that he can be in their life too! I have told many people my story. Many of them were believers in Christ, some had fallen away from Christ and wanted to rededicate to him, and others — my favor-ite — had never known him.

One time we held a youth car wash to raise money for a mission trip. One lady came up to me with a few questions as she waited for her car to be finished. She asked me if I was a Christian. I told her yes. She mockingly said, "You don't *really* believe all that stuff do you?"

I looked at her with a big smile and said, "Well yes, I absolutely do . . . that's why I told you I am a Christian." (I was trying not to be too irritated with her provoking question.)

She told me she was an atheist and that there was no proof of any of the stuff I believed, and that she definitely did not believe all those Bible stories. She said that even if there was a God up there, she had certainly never experienced anything "God-like" before.

"Just because *you* haven't experienced anything 'God-like' does not mean he's not real," I said. "Many people have experienced miracles."

She tried to say there was always a logical answer for so-called miracles and that sometimes there were just coincidences in life. I was excited about my next response because I was about to turn her little thought process upside down. I began to tell her a story. ☺

The first summer Landon and I dated (before we announced our relationship to the church/youth group), he served as the youth pastor at his father's church. His annual youth summer camp was coming up and he asked me to be one of the cabin leaders. I told him no, of course, because I did not feel ready, but he, of course, said I would be great at it. The whole week involved games and competitions between cabins, so I set my mind on winning! (Oh my, that was me for sure!)

As camp began, I began implementing my winning strategy with my cabin of girls, getting them all pumped up for victory. Unfortunately, my back had been killing me all week. My senior year of high school, doctors had discovered I suffered from minor scoliosis in two parts of my spine. At the time, it had pretty much taken me out of all athletic activities. I was in therapy a few times a week as they attempted to straighten out my spine in the hope it would allow me to dodge surgery. Between the awful camp beds and all the activities, my back was in a lot of pain.

In one of the evening services, we had a guest speaker come out to preach. My team and I were seated in the very back row (I had certainly planned it that way). In the middle of the sermon, the preacher stopped and said that God was speaking to him about somebody in the audience with scoliosis, and that he wanted to heal that person. I felt a knot in my stomach and slid down low in my seat. I figured it was probably somebody with a real hunched back or something, but just in case, I wanted to be out of his sight line so he did not call me up! Then he proceeded to get more detailed: "This person has minor scoliosis in two parts of his or her spine and God wants to heal him or her tonight! I'll be patient and wait for you to come up."

He had described my exact diagnosis! *O-M-G!* Suddenly, I felt a little nudge on my back, so I stood up and began to slowly walk down the aisle. It was as if someone were walking me down the aisle. I made it halfway down before freaking out inside, thinking,

What are you doing? I had no clue. I did not even feel as if I had made the decision to get up and walk down to the altar, but I was surely on my way!

The preacher looked me in the eyes when I reached the front and said, "I knew it was you, but I wanted you to make the decision on your own." Then he proceeded to pray over me, asking everyone to reach their hands toward me and to join him in prayer. I felt an incredibly strong power — like nothing I had ever felt before. It was a soft power — if that makes sense — but a liberating power. When they finished praying, I took off running around the tent we were in. I barely remember doing it, but I definitely remember it because I had never done anything like it before. The kids started doing the same and the place went wild! What a night. God had healed me! God stopped the whole service to talk straight to me and heal my back. I remember sleeping very soundly that night! (To top it all off, my girls team beat all twenty teams, including the guys teams, and took first place! I did not play around!)

When I got home from camp I remember running to my mom and telling her I was healed! She said, "What?" I told her the whole story and that I had to go back to the doctors to get another MRI done.

So there I was in the doctor's office, waiting for him to come in and give me the report. He came in, turned the light off, and put two images up on the screen (my before and after). Before he said anything, I could clearly see two different images. In the image of me before camp, I saw two familiar curves in my upper and lower spine. In the image of me taken after camp my spine was completely straight. The doctor said the stretches he had assigned me must have worked very well, but I could tell from the look on his face that he had no real answer for me. Grinning from ear to ear, I told him, "No, it was God!"

After I finished telling this story to the lady at the car wash, I looked her right in the eye and said, "Explain that one for me." She said nothing because there were no gimmicks or coincidences, and there was a clear report from a doctor, so there was no other explanation . . . it was a true miracle. (Acts 4:14: "But since they could see the man who had been healed standing there with them, there was nothing they could say.") I told her that there had to be a higher power, but that I was not there to argue the Bible with her. I wanted to challenge her to think past a limited human perspective to begin to ask and seek where miracles come from. When we acknowledge that miracles happen, we must acknowledge the author of them. Miracles are real and so is God.

She answered me and said, "I have no answer for that one. It sounds like a real miracle. You're a lucky girl." She started to walk away and I shouted after her, "If you keep your heart open, you will experience one too!" She smiled at me and left.

"When we acknowledge that miracles happen, we must acknowledge the author of them."

God has done so much for me, I could go on and on about all he has done! Ultimately, I wanted the rest of my life to be about what I can do and will do for him!

A while back, when I was going through my healing process and beginning to see clearly, I had so many unanswered questions. That is a normal part of the process—to have an aching heart or grieve what is wrong. It is a sign that your heart is working again. After much inner healing I realized I could not go through life questioning and blaming everyone else for my mistakes. I could not allow myself to be bitter towards my dad, toward church people, or toward *anyone*, because in the end, the way I act and live affects the type of *legacy* I will leave.

It took a long time for me to get to the point where I began to think about my legacy. We can get so caught up in blaming others that we end up making all the same mistakes they did, leaving the same kind of legacy—or none. If I blame, I do not take responsibility. If I do not take responsibility, I do not heal. If I do not heal, I leave no legacy. If I leave no legacy, then who am I and who was God in my life? No one will know! I want my kids and their kids to know what God did in my life. I want to leave them an inheritance of love, wisdom, knowledge, and so much more.

Look beyond the circumstances you are in right now and learn to *let go* and *forgive!* Forgiveness will bring you freedom and freedom will bring so much healing! When you receive true healing, you can leave a true legacy.

"When you receive true healing, you can leave a true legacy."

My Familia

Landon and I now live in Austin, Texas, and have two children: a little girl named Payton Olivia Lynn, and her younger brother, Preston Noah Lee. They have been the biggest blessings in our lives. Payton has been worshiping God since she could raise her arms, and dancing and praising him since she could walk. This is the most fulfilling thing a parent can watch! While I was still pregnant with Preston, he had a prophetic word spoken over him; that he would be a "Noah" in his generation and stand for righteousness—even before his middle name was Noah. My children carry purpose, and I am here to help them walk it out and fulfill their destiny. I am already getting to leave a legacy through my children.

We started and own an online network: REVtv.com. It runs 24/7, live streaming young adult programming from reality shows, docudramas, sitcoms, movies, and more that are clean, but cool! We also live stream conferences and special events from around the country. We started the network with the idea in mind that our generation could use it as a platform for their creativity for God's kingdom! If you are gifted in the media field in any way, and want to use these gifts for Jesus and your generation, contact us through the website!

We also travel, speaking all over the world, meeting the most amazing people. I live a blessed life—one for which I am very thankful. I have an amazing marriage and family life. My relationships with all my parents are stronger than ever before. My whole family serves God and loves God.

My mom is a warrior woman, full of wisdom and discernment. She is my best friend and the best Mimi! My mom is Payton's favorite person in the world. I have so much of my mom in me, and I am more than grateful for that.

My stepdad has truly been a father to me, not a stepfather. He has been a huge blessing to our family. I am not sure if we would have made it without him. Whenever there has been chaos (and there has certainly been a lot of that over the years), he was always the calm one who brought peace. He took our whole family on financially, and has always worked hard to give us over and beyond. He is the type of Christian that pulls over behind a bank so no one sees him, and then walks to the street corner to hand money to the homeless person, and never says a word to anyone about it.

My brothers and I have great relationships with one another now. We all know that at any time, if we need one another, we will be there in a second. I cherish the time I spend with all my brothers. They all have unique and amazing purpose in them.

My grandparents are the best. I could never ask for better. Now I get to watch them love Payton and Preston like they did me as a little girl. They have always been the praying grandparents who never lose hope. My parents and grandparents are closer than ever. They have left a legacy of love.

Last but not least, my dad. He has undergone a dramatic life change. Our relationship has never been closer than now. Back in the day, all we had in common were lowly things, but now we can sit around and talk about my life, his life, the Bible, whatever . . . for hours and hours. We have a true love and respect for one another now. I'm so thankful for how much my dad has always loved me. Many fathers use divorce as an opportunity to run and get their freedom back, but mine did not. Regardless of the mistakes he made, my father always loved my brother and I. He has been the picture of what a hard worker truly is. My dad is also very proud of the life I have chosen to live. I am proud of him and love him.

I love my whole family, and am thankful for them for always supporting me in my dreams — including this book! I am proud to have the family I do, and grateful to have seen all that God has done in each of us!

Revolution

I must leave you with this . . .

Having God in your life does not mean life becomes perfect . . . or easy. Yes, my family members are all saved and love God, but it has not been easy and each one would tell you that. It is still not easy. They would all tell you that as well. There have been many ups and downs, trials and triumphs — that is life! At times, I have failed, but I picked myself back up.

We never arrive at a place of perfection. We claim to know this, but then we give up with the first mistake we make. Why? We expected perfection and somehow thought God demanded it. But perfection is unattainable, and pursuit of it leaves us with a life full of disappointments. Instead, we must understand that no one is perfect, but our Savior. He is the one who purposefully died on the cross for us, knowing we were sinners. He did so to forgive us from our sin. He is worthy of our love and we are unworthy of his grace, but it is there for us anyway — if we choose to grab hold of it. I have needed his grace my entire life, but it was only when I decided to receive it and wanted to change that I saw it become powerful in my life. His grace has covered many moments in my Christian walk. In times of marital issues, family arguments, personal growth, and in my relationship with him! His love and grace have covered me.

"He is worthy of our love and we are unworthy of his grace, but it is there for us anyway — if we choose to grab hold of it."

When we were trying to conceive, I had three very devastating reports of miscarriage. The first one hit hard. It was a personal hit to me as a woman, but devastating to think I lost a child. It made me more aware of the abortion issue our country is facing and brought the haunting question to mind: *Why would someone want to get rid of their own flesh and blood?* There I was, trying to conceive with no control over the life inside of me, forced to give birth to a dead baby, and thinking . . . . *There are women choosing this?* They have obviously been deceived by the serpent's voice! If we took a moment to think through things logically and the fact that our society has tried to make us believe it is normal . . . we would turn on society. How can it be "normal" to want to kill our own babies—our future? It makes no sense that anyone, no matter the situation, would want to *kill* their *own* flesh and blood—and the most innocent of innocent beings. If anyone were to have say over life other than God, should it not be the person himself or herself? We are *pretending* it is okay for another human being to choose death for another human being—a baby. That is not okay! We give that decision to the worst of criminals through plea bargains and let them decide how they want to die on death row, so why do the most innocent have no say over their own lives? Can you imagine sentencing a completely innocent person to the death penalty? Of course not! That would be insane. So what is the difference between that person and the living thing inside of us? We are just the carrier of that life, not the owner. God is.

If you are reading this and considering an abortion . . . do not do it. If you feel you cannot take care of that baby, there are plenty of people who will. Please do not choose the death sentence for an innocent. Fear is a powerful thing that can make us do awful things, or keep us from doing the right things. But fear is not real; it is an emotion or feeling. What is real is that baby inside you. Do not get rid of that baby based on fear or any other reason. Seek help and remember that God's power is stronger than any force pressuring you or emotion you may be feeling. Call on him and he will answer you.

If you have already made that decision and chosen to abort your child, please know that God forgives and cleanses us when we ask for his forgiveness. (Just like he did me!) Ask him for forgiveness now and make sure to make a life-change afterward.

Miscarriage was one of the hardest things I ever went through, but it did not shake my faith in God. People ask why bad things happen to good people. It is because we live in an evil world that *man* has corrupted, not God, that these things happen. If people stand firm on making their own decisions and not believing in God, then why do they blame God when something bad happens? I thought they did not believe and it is man's world? In fact, the world is messed up because of evil in man. God is good. But he allows us to make our decisions, like whether or not we choose him. And our decisions do affect others.

We need to be a nation that turns back to God and believes again. Then we will see the fruit of our good decisions. But the next time a bomber or school shooter comes along and kills innocent people, do not question God about why. Instead, blame man's decision and question yourself on the kind of decisions you support and make. Recently I heard plenty of people vent their anger and outrage over a school shooting that had just happened, but then they voted for killing the innocent unborn (pro-choice, so-called). Go figure! It is a cycle America is caught up in. We want our safety and selfish desires granted, but set aside our *morals*. We are deceived. We are no different than a bomber if we are willing to allow women to kill their babies — our babies. We need our morals back. When it comes to morals, it is not about what is "in." Morals are not the fashion of the week for goodness sake. Express yourself with haircuts and clothing — fine — but do not try to take God out of our nation. The problem with doing so seems obvious. The more we try to take God out, the crazier our schools get, the deeper in debt our nation falls, and the higher the crime rate rises! It is time to remove the dark veil from our eyes and stand up for purity again!

I challenge *you* right now . . . bring *purity* back! We need to make purity the "in" thing. America wants blessing while cursing God. That is a double standard. God is the one who blesses, so we must turn back to him and bless his name! I pray that America turns back to God and that the younger generation leads the way! It is time for us to turn from our hurt and pain and use our rebellion in the right way. Rebel against the status quo and societal expectations and stand up for God. The time is now! The call is on you. Be a godly influence at your job, in your family, in the grocery store, at the mall — everywhere. Wherever you are, change it. Be a true leader, one who goes against the norm.

People say they are different but look and behave like everyone else. To be different is not to give away your virginity at prom, to party half of your life away, or to let Hollywood influence you. This will take love, but not a blind love. It will take a love for people and hatred for their sin. People think that to love they must accept another person's lifestyle, and call this *tolerance*. But that is not the truth. Consider the many people who are intolerant toward Christians and God. (Recall the Democratic Party removing God's name from their 2012 convention.) I can love someone, but not what they do. I can bring the love of Christ to them and let God show them *deliverance* that is *real* if they want to accept it. I am not a hater because I want to tell others about true freedom. I have lived both lives and I choose the one I am living now—a free life. I choose Jesus Christ! I choose purity and righteousness. I hope you will too.

Start a *revolution* . . . a revolution of *unscarred*, pure young people who have made it through the battle and who are ready for war. I refuse to carry the scars of my past when God already bore them on the cross for me. If you desire the same unscarred life that millions of young people all over the world and I have experienced, where the old goes away and the new comes (2 Corinthians 5:17), turn the page and pray with me the prayer you find there. Enter this *war* with us!

PRAYER OF SALVATION

God, I desire the unscarred life. I ask for 2 Corinthians 5:17, where you promise to take the old and give me new life. I ask for your forgiveness for all my sins. I forgive myself for the sins I have committed. I believe you died on the cross for me and gave your only Son as my Savior! Thank you for that. I submit my life to whatever process you have for me to help me change to become the man/woman you have called me to be. Help me to be strong in facing temptation and quick to repent if I make a mistake. I desire to please you. I desire to make a difference in this world and give you my life to do with it what you please! Lord, speak to me and mold me. I am yours and I am listening, Lord. Give me wisdom for the times we are in. Help me to have faith and walk it out. I love you, Jesus.

*If you just prayed that prayer . . . you are in! You will spend eternity in heaven with Jesus when you leave this earth, but until then, you just gave God full access into your life to unleash your purpose and destiny! Heaven is rejoicing right now! Start anew and begin to dream like never before. Find a church to plant yourself in (one where you feel the Holy Spirit moving) and let God use you everywhere you go!

All things are possible through Christ Jesus! (Matthew 19:26)

PRAYER OF DELIVERANCE
By Landon Schott

Father, you are Holy, Holy Holy! Jesus, you are Holy, Holy Holy! Spirit of the living God, you are Holy, Holy Holy! Father in heaven

I pray in the name of Jesus. I ask you to deliver me in your righteousness. Just like you saved me by faith, and made me righteous by faith now deliver me by that same faith. I declare no spirit but the Holy Spirit is welcome in my life. (Now say it louder!) I DECLARE, NO SPIRIT BUT THE HOLY SPIRIT IS WELCOME IN MY LIFE. The Lord rebuke you devil and every demonic force that has attacked my life. I do not submit to you any longer! The Lord rebuke you... (list every addiction, bondage and demonic influence that has had you afflicted). Jesus, I need you. I need you to wash me, I need you to cleanse me. I need you to heal me. I need you to free me from all of it. Holy Spirit I submit to you. Lead me, guide me, use my life for your glory! Amen.

ABOUT THE AUTHOR

Heather Schott grew up in the small town of Lake Stevens, Washington, where she met her husband, Landon Schott, at the age of seventeen. They were married on July 16, 2005. Heather has shared her testimony across the country as she and her husband have traveled, preaching the Word of God at conferences, camps, and countless churches.

Heather was raised in a divorced home and became an alcoholic by age fifteen. By age sixteen, she was mixing most hard drugs. She overdosed at age seventeen and was unconscious for three days until she was found in an abandoned apartment.

Over the year that followed, God began to supernaturally change her life. She shares her testimony all over the world, encouraging people with the message that we do not have to live according to our past—Jesus bore our scars for us the day he died on the cross for our sins. Second Corinthians 5:17 says, "Therefore, if anyone is in Christ, the new creation has come: The old has gone, the new is here!" She leads in faith and boldness, believing for healing and deliverance for all who want Jesus.

Heather has a strong passion for the young women of this nation. She preaches purity and fearlessness to be everything God has called them to be, despite the pressures of this world. She also has a huge heart for missions and has been blessed to lead or be a part of many mission trips. Heather loves serving and bringing the truth and love of Jesus Christ to other countries. Jesus says in Mark 16:15 (NLT), "Go into all the world and preach the Good News to everyone."

Heather resides today in Austin, Texas with her husband, Landon Schott, and two children: her daughter Payton Olivia Lynn, and son Preston Noah Lee. In 2012, Heather and Landon started Revtv.com, an online youth/young adult network and media production ministry.

For booking or more information, go to:
info@therev.com
TheRev.com
REVtv.com

Instagram: instagram.com/heatherschott
Twitter: @heather_schott
Facebook: Facebook.com/heatherlynnschott

CPSIA information can be obtained at www.ICGtesting.com
Printed in the USA
BVOW06s2259120216

436578BV00006B/12/P